When Faith Storms the Public Square

Mixing Religion and Politics through Community Organizing to Enhance Our Democracy

When Faith Storms the Public Square

Mixing Religion and Politics through Community Organizing to Enhance Our Democracy

Kendall Clark Baker

Hampshire, England
Cleveland, Ohio

First published by Circle Books, 2011
Circle Books is an imprint of John Hunt Publishing Ltd., Laurel House, Station Approach,
Alresford, Hants, SO24 9JH, UK
office1@o-books.net
www.o-books.com

For distributor details and how to order please visit the 'Ordering' section on our website.

ISBN: 978 1 84694 535 9

A CIP catalogue record for this book is available from the British Library.

Design: Stuart Davies

Printed in the UK by CPI Antony Rowe
Printed in the USA by Offset Paperback Mfrs, Inc

CONTENTS

Kendall Baker's terrific book shows how faith-based community organizing transformed his life and ministry, and how it can revivify the spiritual and civic lives of ministers and congregations alike. When Faith Storms the Public Square *is for all those who care about faith communities, the spiritual health of ministers, or the role of religion in our democratic life.*
Professor Richard Wood, University of New Mexico, author of Faith in Action: Religion, Race, and Democratic Organizing in America

When Faith Storms the Public Square *tells how faith-based community organizing can bring to the table the importance of values for the individual and community. This is essential reading for people who are looking for the root causes behind the current mess in our nation and throughout the world. This book is an insightful tool that can aid pastors and leaders of various faith-based communities not only to teach on social justice issues but also work together to bring about change. Kendall Baker's book should be on seminary reading lists for those preparing for ministry.*
+Phillip Straling, Bishop Emeritus, Catholic Diocese of Reno, Nevada

In these times of undue special interest influence and political demagoguery, Kendall Baker captures for the lay reader the power of faith-based community organizing – a path of faith in action that asserts that democracy demands a government honestly responsive to the people. He argues that 'People of faith... must bring their core values to bear upon the political decisions they make. Not only does the Constitution allow it, but religious conviction requires it.' Kendall Baker tells us why and shows us how.
Attorney Charles Hanson, La Crosse, Wisconsin

Kendall Baker has provided compelling answers to two important questions: "Why do religious institutions need to help empower their people?" and "How do religious institutions go about doing it?" Based on his own experiences he shows how churches and synagogues can be resurrected as their members acquire the skills of community organization. Dr. Baker provides the theoretical and practical foundations for developing programs to bring about positive community change. He shows how disparate congregations CAN unite for change.
Rabbi Hillel Cohn, San Bernardino, California

This timely and thought-provoking book examines the relationship between religious faith and civic life through the lens of faith-based community organizing. Kendall Baker shares his reflections and insights based on many years of experience as a pastor involved in community organizing. In example after example, When Faith Storms the Public Square *demonstrates that community organizing helps promote the common good by helping people find common ground. This book should interest anyone concerned about grass-roots democracy and the role ordinary people play in shaping their own futures.*
Father John Baumann, S.J., co-founder of PICO National Network, Oakland, California

Kendall Baker's timely book is an exceptional resource for church leaders who join in ecumenical and interfaith Community Organizing. Finally we have a foundational text on the religious, biblical and historical roots of organizing! This great read can be used by clergy and lay leaders. It entwines the resources of faith with the principles of organizing and a narrative of real-life ecumenical organizing. When Faith Storms the Public Square *is a must read for every organizer who wants to tap the fundamental passion for justice in American democracy.*
The Rev. Dr. Jane Heckles, national staff, United Church of Christ, Cleveland, Ohio

When Faith Storms the Public Square *is exceptionally insightful and thoughtful as a statement about faith-based community organizing. This outstanding and reflective book challenges the reader to reach into their inner self and to agitate their spiritual center. Dr. Baker writes with great clarity and introspection. Regardless of race or ethnicity, clergy and lay leaders are invited to consider the public policy implications of their belief in a purposeful Creator—namely that life should be lived so as to change our communities, our lives, and our nation.*

The Rev. Heyward D. Wiggins III, Pastor of Camden Bible Tabernacle and clergy leader in Camden Churches Organized for People (CCOP), Camden, New Jersey

This is the book that religious leaders and people of faith must have! Kendall Clark Baker writes out of his own personal experiences as a pastor immersed in community organizing. Baker takes democratic and religious values and guides them through the process of faith-based community organizing. He demonstrates that it is through this formula that families can be directly involved in creating improved communities in the way that God would like them to be. As an organizing pastor I find this book to be a must-have resource that can help enlighten our ministry in building the kingdom of God.

Father Jesus Nieto-Ruiz, Pastor of St. Anthony's Catholic Church and clergy leader in Oakland Community Organizations (OCO), Oakland, California

Rev. Baker's personal stories and in-depth exploration of the religious and secular values at the heart of community organizing are invaluable resources for curious participants and seasoned organizers alike. He provides a solid foundation for leaders and organizers working to build a powerful and informed citizens base standing firmly on this country's great democratic and religious traditions. When Faith Storms the Public Square *is a great contribution … I highly recommend it.*

Joe Chrastil, Lead Organizer, IAF (Industrial Areas Foundation) Northwest, Tukwila, Washington

DEDICATION

To Sonia
and
IDRAR
and
All who have answered the high calling
to be a community organizer

PREFACE

This book is about mixing religion and politics in a powerful way that not only practices democracy, but strengthens it in the process. It is called community organizing. In particular, *When Faith Storms the Public Square* explores from a pastor's perspective the kind of organizing that is rooted in the life of religious congregations.

Faith-based community organizing claims to be driven not by the issue of the day, but by values. I decided to test that hypothesis in my practice of parish ministry. I soon discovered that there is relatively little written on the topic. It seems that community organizing operates mostly by word of mouth.

And so I decided to write about what I was experiencing as I applied organizing concepts to my vocation of pastor. Most that is published on the general topic has been authored by organizers and sociologists and political scientists. When it came to theology, however, for the most part what I found was limited once again to the oral tradition.

What has appealed to me the most about this particular way of mixing religion and politics is the claim that faith-based community organizing is driven by values. But what are those values? Where do they come from? And how do values infuse the organizing activity of religious congregations, in reality and not merely as a slogan?

This book is my attempt to answer those questions. I see this, admittedly only a beginning, as a theology of faith-based community organizing. It is my hope that colleagues and other readers will continue the process of reflecting about their political work from a theological perspective.

I have received help along the way that is so generous it can only be described as grace. Sonia Edwards Baker – who has been my life partner since we were married on the American

Bicentennial, a day we refer to as "Interdependence Day" – has been the primary cheer leader for this book project since its inception. It is thanks to her that I have come even to know what the scriptures refer to as "grace upon grace." My family and friends have held in there for years, enduring countless readings and yet never giving up on me. They have believed in this book project even when my own convictions about completing it have wavered.

I am grateful to friends, colleagues, and parishioners who have critically read evolving drafts and, in addition to encouragement, have offered invaluable suggestions for improving the book. Of particular note are:

David Mann, veteran organizer and United Church of Christ minister. He and I have long labored to develop a strategic approach to the development of clergy engaged in community organizing. It is David who challenged me to come up with a new metaphor (other than Saul Alinsky as "father") to describe the parentage of organizing that is faith-based.

Phillip Straling, Catholic bishop of San Bernardino in the early 1990s. He was the initiator in bringing community organizing to the Inland Empire. Bishop Straling responded to an early draft of my book with strong encouragement and critical suggestions for improving it.

Charles Hanson, attorney in La Crosse, Wisconsin, and former parishioner. Chuck was especially helpful in commenting upon my treatment of U.S. constitutional issues.

Michael Smith, Presbyterian minister and 40-year colleague and friend. I am grateful to Mike for urging me to practice what I preach when it comes to the importance of story. It is thanks to him that I begin my book with a story.

Luther Peterson, professor of Reformation/Renaissance history and friend for almost 70 years. As a scholar, Dr. Peterson is a stickler for accuracy. Thanks to Lute, facts have been checked and rechecked, and citations have been studiously researched.

Richard Wood, sociologist who has written extensively about faith-based community organizing, author of *Faith in Action: Religion, Race, and Democratic Organizing in America*. Professor Wood deserves to be singled out as the one who provided me with the most comprehensive and detailed critique of my basic thesis. I even thank Rich who, as a Catholic layman, saved me, a Protestant pastor, from possible doctrinal error at one key point!

I would be neglectful if I did not also acknowledge two persons from the congregation in Seattle—Admiral Congregational United Church of Christ—that I so enjoy in my retirement. Clay Eals (author of *Steve Goodman: Facing the Music)* helped me immensely in writing a book proposal. He taught me the importance of knowing my audience—in this case the difference between the intended reader of a book and a hoped-for publisher. From his own experience as a successful author, he repeatedly reminded me never to give up but to try, try, and try again. And special thanks to Patti Wunder who designed the graphics found in Part II.

Thanks to last minute assistance from Julie Mullins, a Seattle-based editor, I was able to complete the index on time. And thanks to Lars Larson for taking my author picture.

Finally, thanks to all whom I have been privileged to know who take their respective vocations in religious and political work so seriously. It has been enormously rewarding to be in relationship with community organizers and organizing pastors. *When Faith Storms the Public Square* is the consequence of those relationships. I look forward to continuing this ongoing valuable conversation about mixing religion and politics through faith-based community organizing. Colleagues can join me in testifying to how congregations and personal ministries are strengthened by engaging in faith-based community organizing. And I would like to think also that democracy in America will be the better for it.

Introduction to Part I

WHEN FAITH STORMS THE PUBLIC SQUARE

Religion is in the news these days. No longer relegated exclusively to a private domain, persons of faith have gone public with their concerns. They are working to shape public policy that reflects their values. This book takes the position that the mixing of religion and politics can be either positive or negative with respect to the building of democracy. Like it or not, and for better or worse, faith is storming the public square.

Community organizing is also in the news. Most notable, of course, is the story of Barack Obama, the first American president who was once a community organizer and who drew upon this experience in his campaign. There are even signs of his organizing background in his leadership style as president. In other stories, the controversial effort by some organizers to register voters has drawn the scrutiny of the United States Congress. Only yesterday, it seemed, those familiar with organizing were the relative few who are politically active. Now virtually everyone has heard just enough to have an opinion. Whether adored or abhorred, community organizing has become a force to be reckoned with.

This book is about faith storming the public square through community organizing. This is not, however, the only storm on the political weather front in America today. As this book goes to press the Tea Party Movement, originating in large part as a reaction to President Obama's election and agenda, is causing considerable turbulence. It takes its name from an event leading up to the Revolutionary War, the Boston Tea Party of 1773. Starting out from Old South Congregational Church, an angry crowd protesting "taxation without representation" against the

British crown grew to several thousand colonialists before reaching the harbor where they engaged in a sensational act of civil disobedience. With the subsequent establishment of the United States of America as a constitutionally defined representative democracy, the political relationship with the powers-that-be was dramatically altered—from subject and ruler to citizen and government. Unlike the colonialists in the 18th century, the 21st century tea party participants are actually part of the very government they are protesting against.

Like community organizing, the Tea Party Movement is a manifestation of radical democracy. But the similarities end there. As a grassroots movement of individuals the TPM is an umbrella for a broad range of grievances. Community organizing, by contrast, is based in local voluntary institutions and is highly disciplined in its leadership development, research and formulation of strategy. The former is driven by a narrow set of issues, for the most part considerably to the right of political center, such as reduction of taxes and diminishment of government's role in public life. Faith-based community organizing, on the other hand, is driven not by particular issues, but by values. Government is seen to be a potential ally in addressing concerns of ordinary families. To be sure, the issues identified through the organizing process tend to be progressive, such as affordable housing, access to health care, job opportunities, neighborhood safety, immigration reform and improvement of public education, to name a few. But what drives faith-based organizing is not a partisan agenda or any particular political issue, but unifying values that undergird human community and civic life.

In particular, the argument will be made in this book that one of the most effective and constructive means of bringing faith to bear upon public policy is community organizing. While the mixing of religion and politics in the United States is as old as the story of America itself, the unique strategy and methodology of community organizing is a relatively new phenomenon. When organizing work in the public square is faith-based, religion and politics are being mixed in a new way.

The abrasive idea of faith *storming* the public square will be upsetting to some and pleasing to others. More than hyperbole, this image is descriptive. A definition of storming is "moving angrily or forcefully in a specified direction." In community organizing focused anger resulting from the experience of injustice can be a strong motivation for mobilizing action. Organizing takes power seriously, knowing that change cannot be effected except by forceful intervention. And organizing is highly disciplined, allowing large numbers of diverse peoples to come together around shared values and to move in the same direction in confronting an issue. When politics and religion are mixed in this new way, called faith-based community organizing, the stormy consequence is nothing less than democracy in action.

Although the idea of mixing politics and religion through community organizing will be of interest to many, this book is aimed primarily at clergy and other religious leaders. Those who serve churches that are mainline Protestant, Catholic, historic African-American, and evangelical/Pentecostal, as well as rabbis serving Jewish congregations, and others, will discover a resource in these pages to strengthen congregational life as well as their own personal ministry. Seminary students who envision themselves working in metropolitan areas, first-call pastors struggling to learn how to thrive in ministry, and mid-life pastors seeking to renew and reinvigorate their ministerial vocations will be challenged to think and act in new ways. Denominational leaders and seminary faculty who are responsible for the development of clergy will benefit from these pastoral reflections about church and society. Lay leaders will learn something of what makes their pastors "tick" as well as acquiring tools for helping their congregation bridge the gap between parish life and community need. And community organizers, especially those charged with relating to congregations and their leadership, will gain a better understanding of religious cultures and the challenges/opportunities faced "when faith storms the public square."

There are two parts to this book. The first is a more academic treatment of the topic of the interplay of religion and politics in American democracy. In particular, I argue that there are two primary sources of values informing congregation-based community organizing in America today—democratic and religious. Although the voice in Part I is mostly in the relatively detached third person, it too comes out of my personal history as a lifelong Congregationalist (continuing after 1957 as the United Church of Christ). In community organizing there is a strong emphasis on speaking from lived experience. The dramatic story in chapter 1 that opens this book—Democracy in Action—was an extraordinarily significant event in the life of the congregation I served as pastor. The second half of the chapter expands upon how my participation in faith-based community organizing was a transformative experience in shaping my understanding of pastoral ministry.

Every clergy leader has to contend in some way with the conflicted issue of mixing religion and politics. Some run from it like a plague, others embrace this volatile mix enthusiastically. But there's no avoiding it altogether.

Chapter 2—Mixing Religion and Politics—considers ways in which religion is practiced positively so as to strengthen democracy, as well as to identify religious expressions that undermine the democratic process. Chapter 3—Democracy Under Siege—continues this discussion by examining the threats to democracy from self-serving religion and cultural forces of privatization that erode public life. Faith-based organizing is presented as one significant way to rebuild the community that a vibrant democracy is dependent upon.

Faith-based community organizing claims to be driven by values. It is apparent that those values arise from the religious faith traditions of the participants. What is perhaps less obvious is that there is a pool of values driving community organizing that is shared by virtually every American whether religious or not. Chapter 4—When the People Rule—identifies democratic values arising from the Greek philosophical tradition and modern Enlightenment thinking. Chapter 5—When God Is Sovereign—examines the biblical concept of the kingdom of God and asks how this can be applied in a nation governed as a representative democracy.

The community organizing emphasis on speaking out of lived experience is manifested in reflections upon the religious roots of American political life. This book comes out of the self-interests of my church and family, both of which trace a lineage to 17th century New England Congregationalism. My family's immigration story counts among its ancestors both Pilgrims and Puritans. Chapter 6—Pilgrims and Politics—explores the Mayflower Compact as a uniquely American social contract influencing subsequent understanding of how society can be governed. And chapter 7—Calvin and the Constitution—examines theological assumptions that helped to shape the founding documents of our country. Although personal to me, these reflections coming from one organizing pastor are offered in the hope that others too will find this to be a valuable source for understanding the development of America's national system of governance. I leave it to the reader to balance and expand upon these observations with the invaluable perspective coming from other immigration stories, including the equally needed perspective of original inhabitants.

These reflections on values coming from my own experience are presented here as an invitation to others to engage in this same process. The final two chapters in Part I continue this conversation by singling out four diverse branches of religious faith traditions as sources of value. Chapter 8—A Question of Paternity—begins by challenging the commonplace assumption that Saul Alinsky is the "father" of community organizing. While affirming his indispensable role as an innovative strategist and tactician, another parental metaphor is presented as more appropriate for the approach to organizing that considers itself to be based on faith. This chapter goes on to look at two "ancestors" of faith-based community organizing: the Protestant Social Gospel Movement and Catholic Social Teachings. Chapter 9—More Branches on the Family Tree—continues this theme by considering two more ancestors: the Jewish concept of *Tikkun olam* and African-American Christianity.

It is my hope that readers will examine the values unique to their own faith and shape their civic engagement in the public square accordingly. It is only as this disciplined reflective work is done by each of us that it truthfully can be said of our community organizing that it is driven not by issues, but by values.

The second part of this book is written in the more immediate first person voice. As stated in the introduction to Part II and following, this last section is more directly personal. I refer to it as on-the-job theology, as contrasted with the more abstract armchair variety. This is theology in praxis—theoretical reflection upon the practice of faith-based community organizing from my perspective as a pastor. These final chapters are reflections on the dynamic interplay of the foundational organizing concepts of self-interest, power, relationships, and values, and on the unique clergy role that I refer to as the organizing pastor. Once again, the reader will be challenged to engage in this same reflective process, identifying values unique to one's own life experience and discovering ways to apply these in congregation and community.

One more clarification is in order at this point. The qualifier "faith-based" is used primarily throughout this book for the particular form of community organizing that is explicitly grounded in religious values. This term is not without serious limitations, however. Thanks to the relatively recent faith-based initiatives of President George W. Bush, continued with some alterations by President Barack Obama, the term is frequently associated with a political agenda carried out by a governmental agency. The term "faith-based" is used differently in this book as a way to describe community organizing that is "congregation-based," meaning that it is centered in the life of local churches and synagogues and is driven by the values of these religious congregations. Some organizing networks and religious faith traditions prefer one term over the other. Although the two are used interchangeably throughout this book, my preference is "faith-based." I think it sounds less institutional and more personal, less sociological and more theological. Besides, faith-based community organizing has been in existence long before politicians discovered and popularized the term. To paraphrase an old country western song, organizing was faith-based before faith-based was cool!

Religion and politics are indeed a heady mix. This mixture is what faith-based community organizing essentially is. My hope is that this book will encourage and inform the conversation about how religion and politics might complement one another as a transformative force in public life. And my expectation is that in the years to come this unique mixture called faith-based community organizing will continue to make an indispensable, albeit sometimes stormy, contribution to the strengthening of democracy in America.

Chapter 1

DEMOCRACY IN ACTION

"Surely there is a future, and your hope will not be cut off." [Proverbs 23:18]

The parking lots of Our Lady of the Rosary Cathedral fill rapidly. Soon they are overflowing as a diverse mix of families throughout San Bernardino pour into the neighborhood. Expectations are running so high that no one seems deterred by having to park several blocks away. Like streams flowing together to form a swollen river, a throng of citizens converge from all over the city to take part in what is to be the first "action" of a still young faith-based community organization.

Anticipation has been growing for months. Over a dozen religious congregations have been organizing to address community issues. They represent most every spectrum of the city—Protestant, Catholic, Jewish; Hispanic, African-American, Anglo; affluent, working class, jobless; both westside and eastside of the freeway built years earlier that had succeeded in splitting the population in two, largely along racial and ethnic and economic class lines. Having canvassed neighborhoods to listen to the stories of ordinary families, the congregations are now prepared to present their heartfelt concerns to the Mayor.

San Bernardino had fallen onto hard times with the recent closing of several key industries, including the decommissioning of the local air force base. Once a proud and vital city hailing back to pioneer days, it now is racked with seemingly insurmountable problems: decay of the downtown, loss of jobs, increasing crime, people no longer knowing their neighbors. All the usual elements that make up a litany of a city in decline are present. Prompted by federal statistics annually reporting on cities with populations up to 200,000, a news item on the wires touted the Chamber of Commerce's worst public relations nightmare. "San Bernardino—Murder Capital of the Nation."

Not surprisingly, there is a strong sense that public officials are out of touch. They are alarmingly non-responsive to the interests of ordinary families. The few with money have access to persons in power, but most of the population feel themselves to be disenfranchised. There is in the hazy air a widespread feeling of hopelessness.

But now—June 15, 1994—the time for action has come. Entering the crowded sanctuary, the atmosphere is highly charged. Rather than a traditional service of worship, the mood is more like a political convention blended with a religious revival.

The cathedral chancel has been transformed into a stage filled with leaders from the organizing committee, most of whom are lay members of congregations. They have prepared long and well for this evening's agenda. In recognition of the presence of a large number of Mexican-born residents who speak Spanish in the home as their first language—projections are that the city will be majority Hispanic in little more than a decade—the person who will periodically offer brief translations of the proceedings is introduced.

Words of welcome and an opening prayer are offered by Bishop Phillip Straling who is hosting this event. Then lay leaders call upon the participating congregations to identify themselves. Seated throughout the sanctuary by sections, they are introduced one at a time. As the name of each congregation is announced, members and friends—delegates at this "action"—proudly and enthusiastically stand in unison as the rousing roll call proceeds. *"FIRST CONGREGATIONAL UNITED CHURCH OF CHRIST!"* Almost 100 persons present from this congregation of some 300 members jump to their feet as one, shouting out: *"PRESENT!"* The entire sanctuary breaks out with cheers. Again and again as the roll is called the delegates from the various participating congregations clap and roar and wave their identifying banners. Honored guests who are present in the audience are recognized, including city council and school board members, city and county school superintendents, and other public officials. Scattered "amens" and "halleluias" from the delegates gratefully acknowledge their presence at this action.

Mayor Tom Minor sits on the stage in a lone chair reserved for him. Some of the issues to be addressed go beyond the specific powers of his office, such as public education and administration of justice. Nevertheless, the Mayor has been chosen as the focus of this action since he is the one public official elected by the entire city. Even if an issue lies outside of the City of San Bernardino's sphere of responsibility, the Mayor, as symbol and public leader, is being held accountable for using the power entrusted to him, including his power to influence.

The issue chosen for this action, selected from among the many and diverse problems facing the city, is a concern for youth. There is no question but what this is a priority concern for families. The participating congregations consider this to be a matter of moral urgency. While some issues might have been divisive, this one unites the community.

Research is presented documenting that children and youth are increasingly at risk from crime, falling behind in school, and ill-prepared to enter the job market or college. Most seriously, growing numbers of youth express little hope for their future. Brief testimonies and personal stories are delivered with heartfelt passion by young people and parents.

Next the TOGETHER FOR YOUTH strategy is presented. It had been carefully developed by the participating congregations in the weeks leading up to this action. Articulated in the language of shared values, it is intentionally called a *covenant*. This biblical metaphor referring to the relationship between God and the people of God has been chosen to affirm the seriousness, sacredness even, of the agreement between citizens and their elected leaders to create and sustain human community.

The image in the center of the stage displays a large circle, a "PIE" cut into three pieces—Prevention, Intervention, Enforcement. There are seven innovative programs in all. Prevention includes calling upon the City Parks and Recreation Department to provide supervised late-night hoops on neighborhood basketball courts. An example of Intervention is the development under public school oversight of a program of volunteers tutoring middle school students who have been identified as being at risk of falling behind scholastically. The third slice of the PIE, Enforcement, calls upon the court system to create neighborhood-based, volunteer-staffed Youth Accountability Boards as an alternative to the incarceration of youth for first-time non-violent offenses. Research by the congregations had documented the urgent need to provide an alternative to the current practice of failing to hold youth accountable in the three out of four instances where an overburdened court system has inadequate resources to process youth offenders.

The time finally comes to question the mayor. There is considerable tension in the air. Mayor Minor has been resistant to the idea of such a public gathering. Even though religious leaders of the participating congregations have been working together long and hard in preparing for this action, some relationships are strained as questions arise about how the event might turn out. And congregations are not free of stress either. Members who are personal friends with the mayor's family are having difficulty separating these personal loyalties from their civic responsibility to hold public officials accountable. Nothing like this large and diverse public meeting questioning a public official has ever taken place in San Bernardino. Although the organizing committee has briefed the mayor beforehand about the agenda, including the questions he will be asked, this is clearly not in his comfort zone.

Questions from members of the organizing committee are specific, delivered respectfully but without deference. The purpose is to "pin" the mayor, to have him declare publicly before all the community—and, yes, implicitly before God!—his intent and plan to follow through in seeing that these programs will come to fruition. "Your Honor, will you direct your staff to launch a program of late-night basketball?" "Yes," the mayor replies, "I will order the Parks and Recreation Department to put this program into place." Point by point the covenant is presented, and the promises from the mayor continue to come. "Yes, I will convene the various public school administrators and members of their respective boards to develop a tutoring program for at-risk middle school youth." "Yes, I will work with the judges and the probation department, as well as the city police, to establish neighborhood-based Youth Accountability Boards. " And most importantly, "Yes, I will meet with the organizing committee no later than four months from this moment to evaluate the progress made on the 'Together for Youth Covenant.'"

The long-awaited time finally comes to summarize and seal and celebrate the covenant. Less than an hour has passed since the opening prayer. Suspense is building. The cathedral sanctuary is on the edge of erupting with resolve. A large sign is revealed stating one simple and profound sentence:

WE COVENANT TOGETHER IN SUPPORT OF OUR YOUTH.

A clergy leader briefly summarizes what has been accomplished in this unprecedented civic gathering of people of the community meeting with their elected officials. The unequivocal seriousness of covenant is again emphasized. "The future of our community is at stake," the pastor states with evangelistic fervor. "We have a solemn obligation to provide for our youth, to give them hope. As families of the community, can we do anything less than proclaim, in one voice, our endorsement of this covenant in support of our youth?" A thousand delegates enthusiastically shout out a "YES!" that is heard for blocks beyond the walls of this sacred place. In a spirit of great solemnity, leaders from the organizing committee step forward to sign their names to the covenant on behalf of their congregations. And then, in response to an invitation, all public officials present in the audience come forward to add their signatures to the covenant. Somewhere in the midst of all this holy confusion, Mayor Minor also signs on.

Following a closing prayer, families pour out of the cathedral to return to their homes. There is excitement about a political victory. In this organizing action, San Bernardino has tasted radical democracy. But there is more. People are leaving with hope. Their voices have been heard. For the first time they feel that their troubled city has a future. This organizing event mixing religion and politics is for the families of San Bernardino a tangible sign of hope—a powerful demonstration of democracy in action.

\+ + + + +

The seed for this book had been planted earlier with a question directed to me. Actually, there were two questions at the time. "What is your congregation's self-interest?" Before I could articulate an intelligent response, a few moments later came the second question: "And what is your self-interest as a pastor?"[1]

Pat Kennedy, the first organizer and director for our fledgling faith-based community organization, asked me these questions as we sat in my study at the church. He was making the rounds in his first week on the job, visiting with clergy and lay leaders who had been responsible for hiring him. The questions were disarming, but intriguing. They captured my imagination and started me on a process that has been nothing less than transformational for my congregation, my ministry, and my life.

If that was the seed, the soil was being prepared over the two years prior. When I was considering a move to the First Congregational UCC in San Bernardino in 1990, my curiosity had been piqued by a comment in the church's profile. It stated that the congregation was participating in discussions to launch a new community organizing effort. This sounded gutsy to me, like a church on the cutting edge.

So, during my first week on the job when a member of the church, Helen Bogatin, invited me to attend a community meeting with her, I said yes, of course. A new pastor tends to jump at every invitation like this, glad for the opportunity to get acquainted with the membership and to learn firsthand about the church and the community. It turned out that this was only the second meeting of the newly-established sponsoring committee for a project that would eventually become the Inland Congregations United for Change (ICUC). I met Bishop Phillip Straling, Rabbi Hillel Cohn, Father Robert Miller, several Protestant clergy colleagues, and a number of lay leaders from participating congregations. Clergy and laity were invested in working together to make the community stronger. I was hooked.

I had thought all along I knew what organizing was.[2] But it was not until I struggled with the question of my own self-interest that I really began to grasp what this strange and marvelous creature is that is called faith-based community organizing.

This book comes out of my lifelong experience as a pastor serving congregations of the United Church of Christ. Especially important and rewarding was this last pastorate before retirement when I came to think of myself as an organizing pastor.

Not only did I have the opportunity to benefit from my association with ICUC as it grew into a powerful organization impacting a huge, two-county region, but I have been fortunate to be involved in the clergy development work of the PICO National Network with which the regional organization is affiliated. Originally standing for Pacific Institute for Community Organizations, the network kept the acronym but recently renamed itself to reflect its national and even international scope: People Improving Communities through Organizing. Many of the thoughts expressed in this book will be recognized by clergy and organizing colleagues from the numerous local, regional, statewide and national caucuses we have shared.

After retiring from fulltime pastoral ministry and moving to Seattle, I have had the privilege of further expanding my direct knowledge of community organizing through participating, as a member of Admiral Congregational United Church of Christ, in Sound Alliance. This broad-based community organization made up of labor unions, teacher associations, religious congregations, and other non-profit groups is affiliated with the Industrial Areas Foundation (IAF). While my own personal experience of organizing has been mostly shaped by the faith-based model of PICO, I have been grateful for this opportunity to witness firsthand some of the work that can only be accomplished through an organization broadly-based with a multitude of diverse mediating institutions.

Organizing actions like the one described earlier in this chapter take place again and again in the communities of America. Some are as small as a few dozen citizens presenting demands to the local authorities for a new traffic light at a dangerous crossing where children and the elderly are at risk. Others can include well over a thousand persons coming together from throughout the state to meet with the governor and legislators to address issues of education or health care or immigration or housing. Anyone who has participated in an action can testify to the energy that is released as passion is matched by the disciplined political work of the organizing process.

I wish it could be reported, a decade and a half later, that the organizing action narrated in the opening story turned the city around and that San Bernardino now resembles the New Jerusalem. That is hardly the case, which should not be surprising, given the region's intractable economic problems. There is something about American politics, however, that tends to be messianic in its unrealistic expectations. It is difficult for most persons, perhaps especially so for persons of faith, to embrace the common definition of politics as "the art of compromise." With each public election there is inevitably the disappointment that problems persist under new leadership, especially when the candidate of our choice is way too slow in bringing about a new world order of love and justice and peace, forever and ever, amen.

Although San Bernardino continues to be a troubled city, the story told is nevertheless one of success. Liberal and conservative differences were overcome in establishing programs addressing shared concerns for youth. Some, like Youth Accountability Boards, continue years later to manifest a new partnership between government and volunteers. New relationships were established—between public officials and private citizens, and especially among clergy, leaders, and members of diverse religious congregations. But most importantly, a strong and vital faith-based community organization—Inland Congregations United for Change—was created and continues to be a strong presence in Riverside and San Bernardino counties.

Examples of recent ICUC engagement in public issues include: taking on San Bernardino's towing policy that is unfair to minorities and the poor; a community awareness program of congregations in Riverside displaying banners to promote love, unity, and peace in the face of increased local neo-Nazi activity; fighting in Coachella Valley for improvement and expansion of long-neglected public parks and recreational facilities. Following the organizing principle of never doing for someone what they can do for themselves, there is now a Youth Organizer on staff who, as the title implies, organizes youth to address their own concerns. ICUC is actively engaged in statewide and national organizing initiatives for health care and housing and immigration reforms. But issues come and go. What is most important is that a powerful organization has been established that continues to give voice to the families of California's "Inland Empire" and is a force for democracy through the strong, enduring relationships that have been developed.

It is a good mix when religion and politics come together through community organizing. Personal values grounded in religious congregations take flesh in public policy. When faith storms the public square through community organizing, the result is nothing less than a powerful manifestation of democracy in action.

Chapter 2

MIXING RELIGION AND POLITICS

> *"(Democracy in America) is the result ... of two quite distinct elements, which elsewhere have often been at war but in America have somehow been incorporated into one another and marvelously combined. I allude to the spirit of religion and the spirit of liberty."*
> [Alexis de Tocqueville]

The title of this book points to an obvious question. Precisely how does one go about the task of mixing religion and politics? Clergy are very familiar with the question. The familiar retort is perhaps equally obvious. Very carefully!

Very carefully, indeed. There are some today who argue that religion and politics should be kept entirely separate. That, like oil and water, they don't mix. Any attempt to mix these two volatile spheres of life is doomed to fail, the argument goes. The old adage about never discussing either religion or politics at a dinner party—let alone both at the same time!—is surely not unrelated to the experience of many a social occasion gone awry.

Clergy know intimately, however, that the two have to be contended with. Religious faith is not an exclusively private affair. Beliefs must be put into action, and private convictions must be made public. Likewise, politics in the public square impact upon the life of the believer. The diverse and often conflicting political convictions of members of the congregation present a challenge to every preacher attempting to apply the faith to the world's concerns.

It would be simpler not to mix religion and politics. The attempt to keep the two separate is made by both secular and religious voices. The former are concerned that a particular religious tradition might abuse the political process by attempting to impose its beliefs/values/practices on everyone else, while the latter fear that engagement in the messy world of politics might compromise the integrity of their religious commitments.

There is a degree of truth in each claim. One does not have to look long and far today to find ample examples of religious extremists, whether liberal or conservative, riding roughshod over the opposition. God is on our side, and our side alone, they stridently shout. (Or, in the case of a fundamentalist atheist, Truth is on our side, and our side alone). Other perspectives on public policy can therefore be ignored. When the certainty of religious persuasion deteriorates in this way into uncritical absolutism, there is indeed an argument to be made for keeping religion and politics completely separate.

And there is no shortage of churches appearing to be less interested in providence than in partisan politics. Parishes can be torn apart by activist pastors in pursuit of a political agenda. When a congregation allows itself to be co-opted by partisanship, in effect substituting a political platform for a statement of faith, it has lost its bearings. Again, this distortion of purpose is not limited to any one side of the political spectrum. Whether a parish resembles a Democratic precinct meeting or Republican, it matters little. In either case, when the focus upon its primary religious purpose is dissipated it ceases to have a claim to be taken seriously. Better not to mix religion and politics, the argument goes, than to risk losing one's soul.

The problem is: religion and politics do mix, whether we want it to be so or not. They are obviously mixed together in each person. We do not—cannot—check our religious beliefs at the doorway outside as we enter the voting booth inside. Whether consciously or not, what we believe to be ultimately true and of lasting value informs our political decisions. And what takes place in Washington, D.C. and our state capitols and courthouses and city halls provides a public context in which religious faith is lived out.

Religion and politics also mix big time in America. From the very beginnings of this nation's life politics have been imbued with religion, and vice versa. There is no way to understand American political history apart from religious influences. And the reverse is true also. American religious experience in its diverse manifestations has been uniquely shaped by the political/social experiment of constitutional democracy.

The 21st century is witnessing no departure from this mix of religion and politics in American life. Who would have ever guessed the extent to which religion would play such a central role in the 2008 presidential campaign—what is the candidate's faith, what church does one affiliate with, who is one's pastor?

No, the question is not whether religion and politics should mix. The two have been mixed throughout this nation's history, as they are in the present, and as they will be in the future. [1] The question is rather *how* to mix them.

Nowadays the term "faith-based" has become commonplace. In the United States it has even become fashionable as a generic way to refer to religious activity in general. The concept has been co-opted by politicians for partisan objectives. The Bush 43 presidency established a faith-based initiative, and a governmental bureaucracy to administer it, centered in Washington, D.C. President Obama has continued this initiative and even expanded it by establishing the "Office of Faith-Based and Neighborhood Partnerships." The jury is still out regarding how successful this public policy initiative will be in providing social services on a local level, to say nothing of constitutional concerns about governmental support of religious institutions.

This book considers one answer to the question of how to mix religion and politics in a constructive way that builds democracy. Faith-based community organizing is an intentional mix of religion and politics. As an expression of radical democracy, this political activity is grounded in core values constituting the heart of the American experience. And centered in the life of religious congregations, faith-based community organizing is driven by values that reach back even further than this nation's origins.

Over 25 years ago several networks shifted from the neighborhood-based organizing begun by Saul Alinsky in the late 1930s to a model based on local institutions, such as churches and synagogues and labor unions and professional education associations. Because each of these institutions is a center of values, the political work they engage in through community organizing is grounded in values.

During the 1980s several of the organizing networks—Industrial Areas Foundation (IAF), the PICO National Network (Pacific Institute for Community Organization, the acronym recently renamed as People Improving Communities through Organizing), Gamaliel Foundation, and Direct Action Research Training (DART)—began to emphasize the importance of religious congregations as the setting from which organizing in the larger community can occur. When this political work is centered in communities of faith, then the faith of those congregations has to be taken seriously as the driving force of its community organizing.

Dennis Jacobsen, Lutheran pastor and Director of the Gamaliel National Clergy Caucus, writes of how the local congregation is the building block to community organizing that is "congregation-based" or "faith-based." His writing comes out of his experiences in serving Incarnation Church in inner city Milwaukee. The pastor's central involvement in this style of organizing is essential, Jacobsen says. "Organizing must be linked to the faith and values of the local congregation, to its self-interest, to its needs for leadership training, to the realities of the neighborhood."[2]

Heidi Neumark is another Lutheran pastor who has used

organizing strategies to help the church be effective in responding to the overwhelming needs of its neighbors. She helped found South Bronx Churches, a community organization affiliated with the Industrial Areas Foundation. In *Breathing Spaces* she reflects upon her experiences as pastor of Transfiguration Lutheran Church for 19 years in one of the most challenging contexts for ministry imaginable. Sunday scriptures and traditional symbols of faith come alive as she relates them to the everyday struggles of her parishioners to survive. Neumark writes powerfully and imaginatively about how she and her own family as well as the church are transfigured in the process of building community.[3]

Clergy play a critical role in all faith-based community organizing. Any religious leader of a church or synagogue is sensitive, of necessity, to the possibility that outside groups might wish to co-opt the congregation for their own agenda. Most importantly, pastors are charged with the responsibility to ensure that the congregation's participation in this political work is grounded in the beliefs and values of its respective faith tradition.

The question still remains about oil and water. Are religion and politics in fact a good mix? Or are they more like love and marriage, going together—as the schmaltzy song says—like a horse and carriage?

Many are nervous about this conjunction of the two, and for good reason.

It must be acknowledged that there are many religious voices that do not appreciate the diversity of viewpoints that necessarily constitute a pluralistic society like the United States of America. There is an absolutist approach to religion that cuts across Christian, Muslim, and Jewish traditions, each claiming ultimate sanction for its own narrow view of what constitutes right and wrong, good and evil, truth and falsehood. A quick scan of religious programming on television confronts the viewer with preachers professing America to be a Christian nation, sometimes even claiming that the Constitution says so.

Actually, of course, the founding documents acknowledge nothing of the kind. In fact, it is something quite different they describe. The first amendment states that "Congress shall make no law respecting an establishment of religion, or prohibiting the free exercise thereof." These two interlinked phrases address a creative tension in America's public life. The first makes it clear that the United States is constitutionally secular. Thomas Jefferson, later addressing this question of the non-establishment of a national religion, spoke of "a wall of separation between church and state."[4]

The second phrase of the first sentence in the Bill of Rights makes it equally clear, however, that this "wall" does not prohibit citizens from bringing their faith and values into the public arena. All persons, regardless of religious affiliation or non-affiliation, have the constitutional right to act politically on the basis of their beliefs. This includes not only Christians (or for that matter only a certain brand of Christians), but Jews and Muslims and Buddhists and others. Agnostics and Atheists also have the constitutional right to exercise their beliefs and to act politically on the basis of their values.

At the same time, however, there appears to be a growing number of strident voices in opposition to religious involvement of any sort in the public arena. Whether atheistic or agnostic, they argue that religion is necessarily a destructive and divisive influence in public affairs. Therefore, the argument goes, religious beliefs should be kept private. As with the extreme of religious fundamentalism, this radically secular position would also prevent those of different persuasions from expressing their religious values in the public sphere.

People of faith, however, must bring their core values to bear upon the political decisions they make. Not only does the Constitution allow it, but religious conviction requires it.

Faith-based community organizing appeals simultaneously to both democratic and religious values. Democracy (literally, "rule by the people") exists side by side with religious values. In faith-based organizing it is affirmed that the two are not necessarily in irreconcilable conflict, but actually are complementary to one another. They are not like oil and water, but love and marriage.

Marriage itself, no stranger to communities of faith, is actually a good metaphor to use in reflecting upon this topic. Clergy and religious leaders conduct pre-marital counseling, celebrate and solemnize personal unions, and provide pastoral counseling to persons struggling with their relationships. Like all marriages, the mixing of religion and politics does not come easily or without tension. It has to be worked at and nurtured. Giving attention to boundaries is essential. Mixing religion and politics is not an abstract ideal any more than marriage is, but a living, growing organism.

The radical democracy of faith-based community organizing is considered here as one effective way to marry the two. How? Very carefully, to be sure.

Chapter 3

DEMOCRACY UNDER SIEGE

> *"We must not reassure ourselves with the thought that the barbarians are still far from our gates, for if there are people who allow the torch of enlightenment to be snatched from their grasp, there are others who use their own feet to stomp out its flames."*
> [Alexis de Tocqueville]

The one thing that virtually everyone in the United States can agree on, in principle at least, is the importance of democracy. Whether liberal or conservative, red state or blue, left side of the aisle or right, most everyone affirms the values of the democratic process as a foundation for a superior method of governance.

America has even taken up the banner of encouraging other nations of the world to adopt democracy. Although there is growing disagreement about the effectiveness of military force to impose democracy upon others that have little experience or interest in self-governance, there still appears to be a widespread conviction among Americans that democratic values lie at the heart of what constitutes a right and true political arrangement for the ordering of human life.

In 1831 the French scholar, Alexis de Tocqueville, came to the United States to explore why democratic values seemed to be taking root on these shores more quickly and deeply than in old Europe. His official assignment was to bring back a report on the American penal system, but his personal aspiration was far grander. Traveling to every corner of the United States as it was then constituted east of the Mississippi River, and interviewing more than 200 people along the way, he wrote his two-volume reflection upon the great experiment of democracy still unfolding in the New World. The title, in English: *Democracy in America.*[1] Tocqueville called the progress of democracy a "providential fact," one that depended upon religious faith to keep it vital and to ground it in a mission that affirmed the importance of the human individual living in community.

In the late 20th century and opening years of the 21st, however, many voices of concern have been raised regarding the health of democracy in America. They come from diverse sources.[2] There appears to be an erosion of the ties that bind Americans to one another. There is an important role for religious organizations in helping to reweave the fabric of our society that democracy depends upon.

Religion has not always played a constructive role in the development of democracy, however. There are some mixtures of religion and politics that undermine the development of a strong democratic tradition. Paul David Sholin, a Presbyterian pastor 25 years retired, addresses this concern in a poem. Its title: *"A Twenty-first Century Sonnet."* He compares our new century with the fourteenth, opening with a reference to a late medieval author and his classic collection of one hundred witty and sometimes bawdy tales set against the grim background of the Black Death.

Boccaccio's Decameron *is not read much anymore.*
The century he mirrored—a dark cloud.
Black Death came and covered it with a shroud.
More than half the population was no more.
Survival replaced culture. More in store:
To question or resent was not allowed.
Crusades and Inquisition; threat of war;
Both Church and State threw freedom out the door.

Our century too is threatened with a plague.

Fundamentalist virus is its source.
Religion and the State give it its force.
The threat to peace and justice has been made.
Disaster may be freed to run its course.
Will hope itself fall victim to this curse?[3]

The "virus" of which the pastor-poet speaks is in no way disparaging of any who are clear about the fundamentals of their faith that open them to a world gloriously diverse, filled with compassion, and fraught with future. Rather, the virus threatening peace and justice—core values of democracy—is a narrow and self-serving attitude that undermines community and eats away at a shared hope.

Like a literal virus, fundamentalism is not always easy to see. Historian Martin Marty who has explored this topic in depth observes that "fundamentalist disruption of the American civil order ... tends to take forms that are verbal or gestured—through images in cartoons, disdainful and demeaning remarks, and incivility, all of which make the constructive addressing of social issues more difficult."[4]

This obscurantism conceals the pain experienced by so many Americans today. When families increasingly find it impossible to locate affordable housing... When increasing numbers of our citizens are uninsured and therefore unable to receive essential health care services... When youth are overcrowded into classrooms with inadequate books and supplies and are not receiving the quality education required in order to succeed as an adult in our society... When we lock up growing numbers of our citizenry, even planning ahead by building prisons in anticipation of a future influx... When, in spite of feverish attention given to homeland security, everyone is actually feeling more vulnerable than ever—from the smallest of children to the most senior of our citizens—fearing for our safety in our homes and on our streets and in our schools and in our work places... When these devastating symptoms are experienced on such a large and growing scale by the families of our land, hope itself is at risk.

As dangerous to the world as is the well-known fundamentalism of several religious origins, every bit as dangerous is the political and economic fundamentalism, both left and right, aligned with state power that exploits precious resources, human and material, to serve the few at the expense of the many; that turns its back on the public arena by promoting private greed; and that treats the future as marketable "futures"—a commodity that cynically will be sold to the highest bidder.

Many voices of late have addressed this crisis of hope manifested in the breakdown of community and mistrust of the "other" and the growing gap between rich and poor. One of the clearest statements on this crisis is made in a little book by Andrew Delbanco. It is titled: *The Real American Dream: A Meditation on Hope*.[5] As others have done, this historian relies heavily upon Tocqueville's observations of democracy in America.

Delbanco assumes that human beings need, more than anything else, a sense that their struggles are purposeful, that there is a meaningful future, that there is hope. Against this backdrop he identifies three stages in American history. Each is marked by how it expresses hope—how it provides people with a sense that their lives count for something. The first stage he calls "GOD." Lasting for approximately 200 years from the colonial time of the first European settlers until the establishment of the United States, hope was expressed chiefly through a Christian story that gave meaning to suffering and pleasure alike and promised deliverance from death. The name Delbanco gives to the second stage is "NATION." As Christianity came under pressure from Enlightenment rationality, the promise of self-realization was transformed into the idea of citizenship in a sacred, national union. This second stage began around the time of the American Revolution, continued through the Civil War and even the First and Second World Wars, and did not run its course until the 1960s. The third phase, in which America is deeply mired today, he calls "SELF."

Something died, or at least lay dormant, in the latter years of the 20th century, Delbanco argues. With the loss of transcendence offered by established religion and even that which, however limited, was once provided by the nation, we are left today with only the modern self, an isolated individual, bereft of community and "marooned in a perpetual present, playing alone with its trinkets and baubles."[6]

This increasing privatization of American society has been documented by many. The ugly flip side of this retreat into the private self is a dangerous assault on the value of the public sector. Historian Kevin Starr, when he was state librarian of California, commented upon the state budget crisis as constituting a kind of war—one waged against the larger community apart from which a full human life is not possible. Wanting services without being willing to pay for them, and then justifying this position on the basis of self-centered, private needs, reflects "a contempt for the public sector that constitutes a form of postmodern barbarism: a repudiation of anything that does not seem immediately relevant or useful to one personally, a reconfiguration of society in narcissistic terms."[7]

As tempting as it might be for many people of faith, America cannot turn back the clock to when a belief in God—in particular, an exclusively Christian, and even Protestant and Caucasian, God—provided our society with a unifying story of a purposeful future. Nor can even the sacred union of our nation any longer provide Americans with a shared hope. And it is only too painfully obvious that the isolated, privatized, indulgent Self—cut off from the public arena and disconnected from human community—cannot even begin to substitute for the values needed to provide a substantive societal and soul-saving hope.

The challenge facing America today is to reverse the slippery slide of self-seeking with a commitment to build a community of self-interests. This is what faith-based community organizing is able to accomplish. It is not the only way, of course, but it can help to shape the future of political discourse in America in positive ways. Community organizing is not a panacea for what threatens democracy. But it is a serious approach through which tens of thousands of ordinary families have found access to the political process. Faith-based community organizing is committed to nothing less than reweaving the fabric of America's communities, for that is where hope is birthed and nurtured. Overcoming alienation and nurturing participation in civic life is democracy's best hope. Linking peoples' faith traditions to civic participation strengthens beliefs and reinforces the presence of the sacred in everyday life.

As stated earlier, Alexis de Tocqueville identified religion as playing a vital role in the success of the democratic experiment in America. He paints a nuanced picture, however, acknowledging the possibility of some forms of religious faith as undermining the democratic process. But for the most part, Tocqueville affirms the essential role that religious faith brings to the democratic enterprise because of its commitment to public life and the building of human community. "Religion, by respecting all democratic instincts not hostile to it and by enlisting some of them in its own behalf, successfully struggles against the spirit of individual independence, which is for it the most dangerous."[8]

Faith-based community organizing is a political process, a means of tapping heartfelt values, democratic and religious, to shape public policy. Communities of faith and their religious leadership have a unique and essential role in helping to build and maintain the democracy that lies at the heart of the American experiment.

George Washington appealed to nonsectarian religious

impulses to balance the desire for liberty with a commitment to a national union. In his farewell address as President he drew upon the metaphor of a sacred union to appeal to a contentious people more interested in the former than in the latter. In the face of considerable dissension within his administration that reflected the growing polarization within the public at large, Washington spoke of "the sacred ties which now link together the various parts." Self-interests of the American people were addressed as he put forth the concept of the United States being "an indissoluble community of Interest as *one nation*."[9]

Because religious congregations embody the intersection of public and private, there is no institution in America better suited to respond constructively to the polarization that threatens to tear apart the fabric of our sacred union. As Tocqueville recognized, this relationship between democratic and religious values is not without tension. But when integrated in a manner that does justice to both, as takes place through faith-based community organizing, democracy can become more than a slogan. Religious leaders have a uniquely indispensable role in contributing to the building of democracy.

At a moment in United States history when the democracy of our union was under siege like no time before or since, Abraham Lincoln stated his fervent hope that "government of the people, by the people, and for the people shall not perish from the earth." This is the shared hope of virtually all Americans today as well—that democracy might remain strong and vital and continue indefinitely into the future.

Chapter 4

WHEN THE PEOPLE RULE: DEMOCRATIC VALUES

> *"The New Golden Rule: Respect and uphold society's moral order as you would have society respect and uphold your autonomy to live a full life."*
> [Amitai Etzioni]

Faith-based community organizing is grounded in both democratic values and religious values. They are not one and the same. At points they can even be in tension with one another. Most Americans can lay claim to the democratic values that define the substance of citizenship—such as civic duty, tolerance, fairness, lawfulness, industriousness, national pride. These values undergird the public schools of our land. Religious folk and others will include additional values in the mix, but as Americans there is a common pool of democratic values constituting a foundation for all public life in this country.

In most faith traditions clergy are expected to have a broad background in liberal arts and sciences, as well as in theology. Seminaries and divinity schools commonly require a bachelor's degree or its equivalent before a student is matriculated. This is because of an assumption that congregations and their leadership do not exist in religious cocoons cut off from the larger world. Knowledge of our roots in Western civilization—and, in our global society today, of cultures and religions from the East—is a prerequisite for understanding one's own faith tradition and for the ability to communicate one's beliefs in a pluralistic world.

For starters, preachers are well aware that democracy is not necessarily a biblical value. In fact, the term appears nowhere in the Bible. Democracy has its origins in Greek, not Hebrew, history. It reached its first, and fullest, expression in ancient Athens in the 5th century BCE. To be sure, it was a very limited democracy, since the vast majority of the population—women, slaves, resident aliens, children, and even the elderly—were not defined as citizens and therefore were unable to participate in public decision-making. But the theoretical seeds for democracy were present, as attested most movingly by Pericles around 430 BCE in his famous "Funeral Oration." Quoted by Thucydides in his *History of the Peloponnesian War,* Pericles addressed the citizens of Athens on the occasion of memorializing those of their people who had died in the first year of the war with Sparta. Extolling the virtues of Athenian civilization and governance, Pericles said: "We practice a politics that does not emulate the customs of our neighbors. On the contrary, we are the models, not the imitators, of others. Because we are governed for the many and not for the few, we go by the name of a democracy."[1]

From the very beginnings of modern-day community organizing there has been an implicit recognition of the Greek contribution to political life through a training exercise based upon Thucydides' history of the Peloponnesian War. Virtually everyone undergoing leadership training in all organizing networks participates at some point in a large group role-play based upon "The Melian Conference." Half the group is assigned the role of identifying with the representatives of the people of Melos, a small island off the southeastern coast of Greece, who wish to remain neutral in this tragic war between Athens and Sparta. The other half is given the role of the Athenian generals who have vastly greater military power and whose strategic objectives are to bring the island of Melos into an alliance, whether through persuasion or by force. The text for the role play is Thucydides' own account of the negotiations.

Participants are directed to remain in role as they explore their respective self-interests. The original text raises issues of justice, fair play, honor, freedom, and religion—with each claiming that the gods are on their side. Alternative scenarios are imagined by the participants and dramatically enacted as they each attempt to act from their interests in these negotiations. Finally, the concluding paragraphs from Thucydides' description of how these negotiations actually turned out are distributed. Suffice it to say, perhaps not surprisingly, that the original event didn't turn out well for the Melians in the short run, nor in the very long run of the war for the Athenians either![2]

Why turn to ancient Greek history as the source of a leadership training exercise for community organizing? Why would those who are learning about faith-based organizing in particular—those who, in the words of the old spiritual "ain't gonna study war no more"—take as one of their training texts a history of war that is in fact studied by every person learning to become a professional soldier? The reason is because it is impossible to grasp the meaning of politics apart from the Greek contribution.

The Greeks give us our very language of politics. The word for city or city-state is *polis,* from which are derived familiar English words such as politics, police, policy, polity, metropolis, cosmopolitan. A citizen *(polites)* is a person who participates in public affairs. Citizenship *(politeuma)* refers literally to the commonwealth, the body politic, the public sphere. To be a citizen, therefore, is to be a politician—a political animal. For this reason the notion of a "private citizen" is an oxymoron. The Greek root of the English word "idiot"—*idiotes*—revealingly means "private person."

This Greek emphasis upon the virtue of public life is a central value of democracy. To be fully human is to be political, engaged in the life of the city. Its opposite, a preoccupation with private concerns to the neglect of the larger social order, is ridiculed as a squandered existence. Pericles, continuing in his funeral oration, states the matter clearly: "We are the only people who regard a man who takes no interest in politics to be leading not a quiet life, but a useless one." [3]

Or, as this same thought of Pericles is translated by Thomas Cahill in a way that captures the nuanced meaning of a non-political life: "We differ from other states in regarding the man who keeps aloof from public life not as 'private' but as 'useless.'"[4]

On the face of it, an argument could be made that democracy is relatively value-free. Democracy literally means "rule by the people." Political scientist John Wallach asks: "Can democracy be virtuous? Can virtue be democratic? Can anything common be actually good?" [5] Wallach answers his questions by making an unsettling observation: "From a liberal perspective, in which no political order naturally affirms moral principles, democracy signifies only a system of exercising power—a manner of rule rather than an ethical ideal."[6]

Theoretically, a people could govern themselves in a way in which the rights and wellbeing of minorities are neglected, and majority rule can simply be the vehicle for the privileged to further entrench themselves in self-serving power. As observed earlier, Athenian democracy was actually ruled by a minority, since the vast majority of the population were not considered citizens.

Even when citizenship is extended to virtually all adults—as in the United States today—there is still the risk of what Alexis de Tocqueville named as the "tyranny of the majority." Glenn Tinder points out how Tocqueville anticipated what has come to be called 'mass society'—"society debased by the reign not of tyrants or incompetent kings but of an atomized and degraded people. In a mass society, the people are both oppressors and victims—oppressors because they are sovereign, victims because they are not inherently base but become so in the circumstances created by modern equalization."[7]

So the question is: are there values inherent in *demokratia*, rule of the people? When faith-based community organizing appeals to democratic values, as well as to those arising from the biblical tradition, what in particular is being affirmed?

John Wallach goes on to argue that there are in fact uniquely democratic values expressed in the ancient Athenian experiment. He points particularly to the Greek concept of *arête*, commonly translated as "virtue," signifying a standard of excellence and an example for emulation. "*Arête* was an ideal for performance. It could not be realized by merely holding a belief or expressing a point of view. It needed to be demonstrated in practice."[8]

It is this Greek emphasis upon performance and practice, as opposed to mere ideas and beliefs, that John Dewey articulated throughout his entire career as America's chief interpreter of democracy. As the leading exponent of philosophical pragmatism, Dewey argued persuasively for his conviction that "democracy is freedom." Early on he wrote of the ethical dimensions of democracy. "It is in democracy, the community of ideas and interest through community of action, that the incarnation of God in man becomes a living, present thing, having its ordinary and natural sense."[9]

As Robert Westbrook points out, the kingdom of God on earth for Dewey was not a kingdom at all but an industrial democracy. Although in middle years Dewey moved far beyond his origins in Congregationalism, he never ceased to believe in democracy as a kind of religion with moral impact in education and politics. Near the end of his life Dewey wrote of his faith in democracy as something far greater than external political machinery, but as a way of life to be practiced. "Democracy is a way of personal life controlled not merely by faith in human nature in general, but by faith in the capacity of human beings for intelligent judgment and action if proper conditions are furnished."[10]

Democracy, arising from Greek culture, is in fact value-based. Pericles went on to identify several qualities, or virtues, that distinguished the Athenian democracy from its cultural and political and economic nemesis, Sparta: toleration of diverse styles of life, free and open relations among each other, and generosity of spirit. In commenting upon the Funeral Oration, Thucydides testified "how each individual is interested not only in his own affairs but in the affairs of the state as well. Even those who are most occupied with their own business are extremely well informed on general politics. This is a peculiarity of ours: we do not say that a man who takes no interest in politics is a man who minds his own business; we say that he has no business here at all!"[11]

In other words, the key democratic value informing faith-based community organizing is an affirmation of the public life as essential to the human spirit. There are strong individualistic forces in American life today that oppose this value. Politicians who personally invest in public life are generally not held in high esteem. Some who hold public office themselves cynically denigrate the importance of government—even though they have striven through election or appointment to become the government! Private concerns commonly trump a commitment to the public sphere. But, in contrast to these strong negative tendencies in modern America, the Greek democratic tradition affirms as a core value the vital importance of politics.

Plato referred to this as the democratic capacity to practice the art of politics *(politike techne)*. Speaking through the character of Protagoras, he distinguishes between private conversation (including professional discourse among specialists) and public discourse, arguing that with the latter every single citizen has the authority to contribute. "When the debate involves political excellence *(arête)*, which must proceed entirely from justice and temperance, they accept advice from anyone, and with good reason, for they think that this particular issue, political or civic virtue *(arête)* is shared by all, or there wouldn't be any cities."[12]

Tolerance, in other words, is a key democratic value. The Greeks knew that it is essential in order for public life to function. This capacity to recognize and respect the rights, beliefs, and practices of others—affirming the importance, even, of dissent and disagreement—is a core value underlying the Greek understanding of reality.

In identifying tolerance as a democratic value, honesty requires an acknowledgement that this is not a biblical value. Nor is it, generally speaking, a religious value. The nature of religious faith is the making of truth claims. Life is too serious not to hold convictions about what is ultimately true. How can one respect, let alone tolerate, that which is considered falsehood and error? The apocryphal observation of G.K. Chesterton, "Tolerance is the virtue of the man without convictions," summarizes well religious antipathy to this democratic value.[13]

The few references to tolerance in the English Bible are all negative. In the Book of Esther, Haman attempts to persuade King Ahasuerus that the Jews should be annihilated because "their laws are different from those of every other people...so that it is not appropriate for the king to tolerate them." [Esther 3:8] Jesus says that it will be more tolerable for Sodom and Gomorrah (which were destroyed) than for cities that reject his message. [Matthew 10:15] And at the end of history, the Risen Christ criticizes the members of the church in Thyatira (located, similar to ancient Athens, in the syncretistic environment of Hellenistic culture) who, in spite of their many good qualities, are putting up with evil influences. "I have this against you: you tolerate that (false prophet) Jezebel." [Revelation 2:20]

To be sure, there are complementary biblical values that contribute positively to civic life, such as hospitality. Welcoming the stranger—the one who is 'other'—lies at the heart of the biblical witness. It can even be claimed that *acceptance,* receiving something or someone with gladness, is a biblical value. But the same cannot be said of tolerance. It is thanks to the ancient Greeks, and not to the Hebrews, that we are encouraged to embrace diversity and coexist with those who believe and act differently than ourselves.

Clergy sometimes mistakenly believe that only biblical values are worthy of being affirmed. The truth is, however, as every effective preacher knows, the religious message of the day is always embedded in an ocean of shared cultural values that the congregation swims in. Some of those secular values, old as the Bible but from other sources, are foundational for Western civilization. Without the Greek contribution, democratic discourse would be impossible. Western culture is shaped by both Greek and Hebrew worldviews. In affirming democratic values as one of the sources for faith-based organizing, tolerance of those holding different beliefs is a foundational conviction in allowing congregations to work side-by-side with one another—gladly even!—in addressing shared concerns for public life.

Chapter 5

WHEN GOD IS SOVEREIGN: BIBLICAL VALUES

"Listen to the voice of the people in all that they say to you; for they have not rejected you, but they have rejected me from being king over them."
[First Samuel 8:7]

As important as are democratic values for all who are privileged to live in a nation where "the people rule," people of faith rely also upon a higher power to inform their participation in the public arena. It is not enough for the religious faithful to ask what do the people want. Another question must be asked as well: What does God want?

Even for persons who do not consider themselves religious and who are skeptical about claims to know the will of God, if one wants to understand American political life it is essential to have some awareness of the contribution made by religion, originally, and presently, in shaping the United States. Democracy in America is a child both of the Enlightenment and of the Bible. As argued in the last chapter, this country's origins have been profoundly influenced by Greek culture. But another tradition, quite different, that has impacted upon Western civilization in general and America in particular is the Hebrew world of the Bible. To claim that faith-based community organizing is grounded in both democratic values and biblical values is to recognize this dual parentage by Greek and Hebrew origins.

Clergy, by training and practice, tend to be relatively more at home, or at least equally at home, with this latter tradition.

Years of academic study in Bible, theology, history, ethics, worship, and preaching set pastors apart from the population at large through their familiarity with this particular body of knowledge. And the daily practice of celebrating sacred story in worship and preaching, as well as teaching doctrine and spiritual development, providing pastoral care, and personal disciplines of prayer and study, add up to a perspective on public life that is unique. Religious leaders ask not only what do the people want, but what does God will? The Bible in which God is the protagonist, therefore, is a foundational source of values for faith-based community organizing.

The history of the West is a synthesis of Greek and Hebrew cultures. Rabbinic Judaism has kept the Hebrew witness of the Bible alive in the Western world, especially when the church too often has been ambivalent about its essential Hebraic roots. But it is the Christian Church, as the religion of the majority from the time of Constantine in the 4th century on into the modern age, through its co-opting of the Hebrew Scriptures as its Old Testament, that has ensured the public influence of the biblical story in western civilization.

It is reliance upon the biblical story that sets religious congregations apart from other mediating institutions such as unions and professional educational associations. All are based in values arising from their respective histories and functions in society. But for religious institutions the Scriptures are affirmed as a central source of values. Indeed, it is the biblical story, as each faith tradition interprets and reenacts it, that is considered normative for the life of synagogue and church. Worship for Jews is centered in systematic reading and scholarly interpretation of the sacred story. Throughout the year this narrative is ritually reenacted, as in the family *seder* meal during Passover *(pesach)* when the powerful events of liberation from slavery and the becoming of God's people is told and acted out. Worship for Christians is through Word and Sacrament as the sacred story of

God's covenant in Jesus Christ is preached from the pulpit and dramatically enacted at the table. Communion with God through prayer, collectively in public worship and individually through private devotion, is essential for people of faith. These solemn rites that are repeated daily, weekly, and seasonally bind the people of God to one another, creating a strong sense of identity and solidarity. The values arising from these ritual acts are a powerful source for guiding and inspiring the political work of people who share the biblical story.

One can turn to many different sources in the Bible to identify core values of religious faith traditions relating to these sacred stories: the creation narratives and the patriarchal history; the exodus story of liberation from slavery and subsequent sojourn in the wilderness; the exile into Babylonian captivity and eventual return to rebuild the shattered nation. There is the rich prophetic tradition of Isaiah and Jeremiah and Ezekiel, as well as the shorter books by Amos and Hosea and others. The Wisdom literature of the Psalms and Proverbs and Job and others can be mined for meaning. In the New Testament the Gospels and the Pauline epistles, especially for Christians, are profound sources for reflecting upon the values that guide and drive the organizing process. The opportunities are virtually unlimited for finding texts that inform and ground the political work of religious congregations.

There is one particular biblical story, however, that stands out as paradigmatic for the topic of mixing religion and politics. In telling of the institution of the monarchy, First Samuel 8 describes the tension between two conflicting views of manifesting God's sovereign rule within history.

Central to the biblical story is an affirmation of the sovereignty of God. The notion of sovereignty being located in the people, as is the case with the Greek understanding of democracy, is foreign to the Bible. The prayer Jesus taught to his disciples, and which is repeated in virtually every Christian church at least weekly, asks of God: "Thy kingdom come, thy will be done, on earth as it is in heaven."

At first glance this might sound like a recipe for theocracy. Such a viewpoint, however, does not necessarily lead to theocratic governance. The biblical story is highly nuanced concerning the issue of how "kingdoms" should be organized in this world. In fact, the biblical witness contains conflicting visions of what constitutes right governance.

This was playfully, yet seriously, demonstrated in a local clergy caucus in San Bernardino. Several religious leaders—Protestant, Catholic, and Jewish—who were engaged in faith-based organizing decided to spend an entire day in reflecting theologically upon shared concerns for the community. Based upon the story of Samuel and Saul, a role play had been developed called "The Great Debate" in which the group was divided with half taking one side or the other of the two contrasting approaches to governance found in First Samuel. One group called themselves "The Prophetic Party," and the other "The Kingly Kluster." A Catholic priest, Fr. Bob Miller, and a United Church of Christ minister, yours truly, took opposite roles from the stereotype of their respective faith traditions—at least with respect to their polity, or ecclesiastical governance. The Catholic pastor coming from a hierarchical polity that literally draws upon monarchical symbols argued for the prophetic, while the Protestant pastor coming from the radically democratic background of Congregationalism argued for the monarchy. As expected, the results of this role play were inconclusive. But participants left with a greater understanding of the ambiguities of contrasting governing systems and the resolve to bring their values to bear by working pragmatically through the mundane governing officials back home—namely the Mayor and City Council.

The story of the origin of kingship in the life of ancient Israel dramatically addresses this tension about what is considered to be good and faithful governance. When Canaan was settled following the exodus from Egypt and sojourn in the Sinai wilderness late in the 13th century BCE, there was no centralized government. The twelve tribes were loosely knit together in a confederacy ruled by charismatic (spirit-filled) leaders that are commonly called today, somewhat erroneously, judges. Scholars refer to this period as the *amphictyony*, a Greek term referring to neighbors. Each tribe was autonomous in this decentralized form of governance. They came together only on occasion to fight a common enemy or to renew their covenant based upon a shared religious heritage acknowledging that God alone was sovereign.

After almost two centuries of being ruled by tribal judges, the last of whom was Samuel, the people finally demanded a king. This dramatic story tells of how the elders of Israel came together to express their displeasure with Samuel's leadership, especially as it was practiced by his corrupt sons, demanding that they be given "a king to govern us, like other nations." As the story unfolds, this request is interpreted as a rejection not only of Samuel as a judge, but of God as their king. God tells Samuel that he should nevertheless go along with their foolish and faithless demands. "Listen to the voice of the people in all that they say to you; for they have not rejected you, but they have rejected me from being king over them."

Every decision has consequences, however, so God tells Samuel to let the people know what will happen as a result of their choice. "These will be the ways of the king who will reign over you: he will take your sons and appoint them to his chariots and to be his horsemen, and to run before his chariots." This was conscription, or the institution of the draft as it would come to be called many centuries later. "Some will plow his ground and reap his harvest, and will make his implements of war and the equipment of his chariots." President Eisenhower at a much later time would refer to an exaggerated form of this as the "military-industrial complex." The list of painful consequences goes on and on. "He will take the best of your fields and vineyards and olive orchards ... and the best of your cattle and donkeys ... and a tenth of your flocks, and you shall be his slaves." Taxes, anyone? Well, God concludes in so many words, you can have your human king. But just don't come complaining to me about it afterward. "In that day you will cry out because of your king, whom you have chosen for yourselves; but the LORD will not answer you in that day."

The response of the elders to this warning is telling. Turning their back on Samuel's counsel, they say, "No! But we are determined to have a king over us, so that we also may be like other nations, and that our king may govern us and go out before us and fight our battles."

Saul becomes their first king, followed by David and Solomon and a host of others. Each of them, to some degree, bears out the warning delivered by Samuel. Only God, according to the prophetic tradition, is worthy of being king. And every human attempt at providing a substitute is programmed for disaster.

There is another biblical tradition, however, that stands in direct opposition to this negative portrayal of the human institution of the monarchy. Chapter 9 tells Saul's story, how he was "a handsome young man ... (who) stood head and shoulders above everyone else." [9:2] God speaks very differently in this chapter as Saul's virtues are extolled. "He shall save my people from the hand of the Philistines; for I have seen the suffering of my people, because their outcry has come to me." [9:16] Chapter 10 begins with Saul being anointed by God as ruler over Israel with the command "to reign over the people of the LORD and to save them from the hand of their enemies all around." [10:1]

Students of the Bible know that God speaks through many human voices, some of them in apparent contradiction to the others. Scholars identify the several sources lying behind the text as we have it today, conjecturing how editors in subsequent years would weave stories together to create one larger narrative. These stories of the origin of kingship in ancient Israel are one obvious example of this process.

One way of understanding the larger biblical story, found in the Hebrew scriptures and in the Christian New Testament as well, is to discern conflicting viewpoints about governance. The prophets, speaking in the name of God, railed against the abuses of the kings. Elijah predicting the downfall of King Ahab is but one example. "Because you have sold yourself to do what is evil in the sight of the LORD, I will bring disaster on you; I will consume you and cut off from Ahab every male, bond or free, in Israel." [First Kings 21:20 ff.] During the time of the monarchy, on the other hand, there also arose a hope that God would someday send an ideal king. The rite of installing a monarch was through anointment with oil, literally making every king a messiah (from the Hebrew *masiah,* meaning anointed). Inevitably, virtually every actual king turned out to be a great disappointment. So the prophetic expectation grew that the day would come when God's intentions for history would be accomplished through the agent of an ideal messiah. As Isaiah prophesied: "His authority shall grow continually, and there shall be endless peace for the throne of David and his kingdom." [Isaiah 9:7]

Even the early Christian witness reflects differing perspectives about who Jesus is as one who lived out a vision of the kingdom of God. Is Jesus the ideal messiah—a new king—in the tradition of King David? Simon Peter, in response to Jesus asking who people are thinking he is, says so: "You are the Messiah!" [Mark 8:29] Or is Jesus a prophet in the tradition of Elijah? In the Gospel of Mark, at least, Jesus himself seems to be reluctant to embrace a messianic identity. His immediate response to Peter's confession was to sternly order the disciples not to tell this to anyone. In the next chapter Jesus speaks in a way that identifies himself with a biblical archetype of the prophetic vocation: "Elijah is indeed coming first to restore all things. How then is it written about the Son of Man, that he is to go through many sufferings and be treated with contempt?" [Mark 9:12]

In the development of the early church following the ministry of Jesus the same tension is played out between the prophetic and the monarchical visions of how to govern. Are Christians to be primarily a Pentecost people ruled directly by the prophetic spirit? [Acts 2] Or are they to understand themselves as obedient citizens called to "accept the authority of every human institution, whether of the emperor as supreme, or of governors, as sent by the Lord, to punish those who do wrong and to praise those who do right?" [First Peter 2:13; see also Romans 13:1-7]

Indeed, the subsequent history of the church itself can be read as a story of contradictory visions of governance. The conflict during the 16th century Reformation, in addition to ritual and theology, regarded the question of authority. This tension is manifested within each of these faith traditions as well. Religious orders commonly arose as a reform movement within the Catholic Church, obedient to Rome yet sometimes espousing an alternative vision of the religious life. And in Protestantism the full range of prophetic versus kingly is manifested in a multitude of denominations affirming different polities, or governance—from those on the prophetic side coming out of the Radical Reformation, to those on the monarchical side that order the life of the church through the episcopacy.

As "The Great Debate" of the clergy caucus had demonstrated, there is no single viewpoint to be found in the Bible about political governance. In spite of some television preachers who would claim otherwise, there is not to be found in the Bible nor in the history of the church following any single approach as to how societies should organize themselves politically.

What is central, however, is a conviction that God is sovereign lord over all of history and creation. Although the actual phrase "kingdom of God" is virtually missing from the Hebrew scriptures, the concept is nevertheless deeply rooted throughout. Jesus took this metaphor as the primary way to express his vision. He begins his public ministry with an announcement: "The time is fulfilled, and the kingdom of God has come near; repent, and believe in the good news." [Mark 1:15]

In English, the term "kingdom" usually refers to a spatial territory with boundaries over which kingly authority is exercised. But the Greek word for kingdom, *basileia,* attempting to translate the Hebrew word *malkuth,* points more to a social reality. It is the active sphere in which life is ordered according to God's intentions. "Set in this context of extolling God as King, it is evident that *malkuth* is a verbal noun of action, describing the effective exercise by God of his kingly authority and power."[1]

Jesus taught that the kingdom of God is what is eternally true. At the end of time, the reign of God will be the fulfillment of history. For Jesus, however, the coming reign of God is imminent and not relegated to some impossibly remote future moment. And it is immanent, manifested in the here and now within history through faithful human response. "The kingdom of God has come near." Or as some biblical versions state it, "The kingdom of God is at hand." It is within reach. New Testament theologian Krister Stendahl coined the phrase "eschatological itch" to refer to this sense of urgency and intense expectation. Vision implies seeing ahead, discerning a future reality. Jesus affirmed that this future reign, through repentance and trusting in the good news of God, was breaking into the present.

"Kingdom of God" is obviously both a political metaphor and a religious one. It is political, in the sense of referring to the ordering of society. And it is religious, in that it refers to God's reign, rather than to human rule.

Jesus chose this political and religious metaphor of God's kingdom as his primary way of articulating his vision for human society and how human relationships should be lived—not in some distant future on the other side of history, but within history. To speak of the kingdom of God is a statement of values expressing the way that life is to be lived and ordered in the here and now. To be sure, there is Caesar and all his minions, and their rule must be taken seriously as the political-historical context in which life is lived on earth. But it is God's rule of justice-love that is ultimately important. To speak of God's kingdom in contrast with Caesar's kingdom is to point to the world as God intends it to be—the way within human history that economic resources are to be allocated and fiscal priorities are to be established and political decisions are to be made.

While the Bible offers no single blueprint for governance, the God of biblical faith is not impartial when it comes to dealing with the sufferings of human beings. God can never be claimed exclusively by any particular political ideology, whether conservative or liberal. God is certainly not in the corner of either the Democratic or Republican parties. Nevertheless, the biblical witness affirms that God is not neutral or balanced when it comes to weighing the scales of justice between rich and poor. Rather than being blindfolded like the Greek symbol of Lady Justice, the Hebrew God metes out justice with eyes wide open, caring for the poor, the weak, the marginal. As Old Testament theologian Walter Brueggemann writes: "Yahweh is known to be a resilient and relentless advocate of and agent for justice, which entails the complete reordering of power arrangements in the earth... The intention of Mosaic justice is to redistribute social goods and social power; thus it is distributive justice."[2]

Christians pray repeatedly that the kingdom of God might come, that God's will be done on earth as in heaven. Although the particular phraseology of this prayer belongs to Jesus, it expresses a vision that is shared in large part by Jews and Muslims and others. God is sovereign lord over all of life. For a person to pray for the coming of the kingdom of God on earth as in heaven, one is expressing a hope that justice-love will be manifested—in history as in eternity, in flesh and blood as in spirit, in public as in private, in politics as in religion, right here and now in this messy world in which power is pitted against power and where families of our country are struggling to survive.

Religious congregations can never be content with asking only what the people want, as essential as this is. But, with the prompting of their leadership, they must also prayerfully ask: what is the will of God? Clergy know that democracy-building for people of faith is grounded not only in Enlightenment values, but also in prophetic values. Therefore, faith-based community organizing is permeated with a biblical vision of distributive justice. Democracy can never be allowed to deteriorate into a system of might makes right. Because, when it comes to acting politically, a congregation's eyes, like God's, must also be wide open.

Chapter 6

PILGRIMS AND POLITICS

"We could not stand the stench inside if it were not for the storm outside."

[Reinhold Niebuhr in likening the church to Noah's ark, but equally apropos to the Mayflower.]

When Alexis de Tocqueville arrived in the United States, he commented upon how the country's religious aspect first captured his attention. He contrasted the synthesis of religion and democracy in America to the antithetical opposition of religion and governance occurring in old Europe at the end of the 18th century—especially as he had observed the violent unfolding of the democratic revolution in his own native France. In looking at America he saw how essential the role of religion was in shaping the uniqueness of the modern democratic experiment. He noted how religion in the United States, although never intervening directly in government, must be considered "the first of America's political institutions."[1]

Faith-based community organizing takes seriously this observation by Tocqueville. Congregations are not only religious institutions but, from the very beginnings of America to the present day, they have also played an essential role as political institutions—not through partisanship (at least when First Amendment sensibilities are observed), but as an organized spiritual and moral force providing core values to women and men participating in the shaping of public policy.

In contrast to Europe, however, where a single church most commonly was identified with governmental power, what is notable in America is the immense diversity of religious practice from colonial origins to these opening years of the 21st century. From the beginning of America's national story, religion has been more than the private expression of individuals. It has been individuals gathered together in community, in the "voluntary organization" (Tocqueville's term) called congregation and countless religiously-directed groups. As the authors of *Religion in American Life* state, "The story of religion in America thus stands at the heart of the story of America itself. ... [This] is not an aberrant story. In a society so remarkably secular in so many ways—the American pursuit of wealth, the quest for international leadership, the love of science and technology—religion frequently stood at the heart of the American experience itself, guiding it, underscoring its central themes, providing its often most idealistic—and sometimes its most difficult—expressions. Indeed, religion's centrality to twenty-first century America—especially its complexity and intricacy—is a virtual invitation to understand the rich and fascinating evolution of religion in the American past."[2]

Clergy and their congregations are frequently ambivalent about the role of religion in public life. Some seem happy to embrace politics uncritically, while others are more comfortable keeping a safe distance by avoiding involvement in controversial public issues. The thesis of this book, however, is that religion is in fact "a political institution" and that people of faith must find responsible and effective ways of bringing their faith to bear upon public life.

One such way is to explore the contribution of one's own faith tradition to the larger American story. Every religious leader today has a story to tell of how their ancestors came to these shores, if they were not here already, and how they helped to shape this country. Embedded in the stories that each of us can tell are the values that drive our participation in the public arena. As with every human story, there are "skeletons" we would rather ignore, shameful incidents prompting a degree of humility at the least and hopefully even an act of contrition. What follows is one such story coming from the author's family and church history. It is told here not only in the hope that it offers a valuable perspective in its own right that might be beneficial to those from other faith traditions, but also as an example of how all religious leaders can discern the unique values driving political engagement through the telling of their own stories.

Reaching back to the beginnings of colonial history, the Pilgrims who came from England on the Mayflower are best known through the American story of what is commonly called "The First Thanksgiving." This tale of a great feast shared by immigrants and natives is a national myth of origins. The tranquility was not to last among the Pilgrims themselves, to say nothing of their subsequent treatment of their native hosts who had befriended these innocents from Europe. [3] Nevertheless, as a myth of origins it has its place in reminding Americans of who, in our better nature, we aspire to be as a diverse people sharing a world both old and new.

Less known, however, is the historical account of what constitutes the most significant contribution of the Pilgrims to American democracy—the establishment of the Mayflower Compact. This legal agreement was unique in the New World by creating the first American settlement based on a social contract. Tocqueville cites this contract as one of the founding documents of what was to become the United States.

The two-month voyage across the Atlantic had been arduous, not only because of the weather and crowded conditions on a small ship (about 104 feet in length—little more than three first downs in a Thanksgiving football game), but especially because the passengers did not get along well with one another. It is often claimed that the primary purpose of this voyage was to escape oppression in the search of religious liberty. For some that was the case, but for most of the passengers it was economic opportunity that prompted signing on for this trip. About a third of the 100 or so men, women and children had come for exclusively religious reasons—a small Separatist church in search of freedom to worship as they chose. The remaining 66 passengers, also Christians but without dissenting from the established Church of England, were motivated primarily by commercial interests. The former would huddle on deck for prayers, turning their backs on the others, referring to themselves as "Saints" and to the others as "Strangers." The conflict was so severe the entire enterprise was at risk. "Mutiny on the Mayflower," one historian has called it. This did not bode well for a successful settlement in a new world that was hostile to their aspirations.[4]

As the Mayflower sat in harbor off Cape Cod with the threat of winter descending, it became apparent to all that they would not survive unless they found a way to band together. The necessity of reaching agreement was all the greater because their charter from the King of England giving them legal authorization to settle was for a location several hundred miles to the south. Before they disembarked, the Pilgrims—a term first coined over two centuries later, in 1840, to refer to the combined passenger list of "Saints" and "Strangers" alike—wrote an agreement for the temporary governance of the colony. On November 11, 1620, 41 men signed what came to be known as the Mayflower Compact. (As in ancient democratic Greece, men were presumed to be able to speak for women, as well as for children.) The signatories included not only the leaders from both camps, but most importantly cut across lines of social class—also including hired men and some of the indentured servants.[5]

The Mayflower Compact drew upon two traditions: the biblical concept of covenant central to the theology of John Calvin, expanded from its original understanding as a relationship between God and human communities to apply also to political agreements among persons within those communities; and the philosophical concept of social contract in the 17th century developed by political philosophers Thomas Hobbes and John Locke. This social contract was based upon the belief that for a government to be legitimate it must derive from the consent of the governed. The Pilgrims promised in writing and under their signatures that they would *"solemnly and mutually in the presence of God and one another, covenant, and combine ourselves together into a civil body politic, for our better ordering and preservation ... and by virtue hereof to enact, constitute, and frame such just and equal Laws, Ordinances, acts, constitutions, offices from time to time, as shall be thought most meet and convenient for the general good of the Colony, unto which we promise all due submission and obedience."*[6]

In 1802, almost two centuries later, John Quincy Adams gave an address at the annual Forefathers' Day celebration in Plymouth, Massachusetts. He spoke of the Mayflower Compact as the primary contribution of the Pilgrims to American democracy. "This is perhaps the only instance in human history of that positive, original social compact, which speculative philosophers have imagined as the only legitimate source of government. Here was a unanimous and personal assent by all the individuals of the community to the association by which they become a nation."[7]

Perhaps not surprising in a speech by a politician at a patriotic occasion such as this, there is some hyperbole. The decision to sign the agreement was not, in fact, unanimous. Although most of the male passengers signed on, all did not. Women, as mentioned earlier, were not invited to sign. But the point remains that the overwhelming majority of the Pilgrim families did sign the agreement, and those signing represented the full diversity of religious and economic and class interests.

The Separatist contingent of the Mayflower, having lived for over a decade in Leyden, Holland, before setting sail for America, had been strongly influenced by the covenant theology of John Calvin that was so dominant in continental Europe in the early 17th century. This settlement at Plymouth remained relatively small, however, with the remaining years of the 1620s seeing only a few hundred additional immigrants from England settling nearby. It was not until 1629, when the Massachusetts Bay Colony was chartered, that "The Great Migration" began.

These new settlers were English Puritans. Like the Pilgrims, they too were steeped in Calvinism. Unlike the Separatists, however, they stayed inside the Church of England with the intent of "purifying" it from what they considered to be the ritualistic excesses of Catholicism. Between 1629 and 1650 over 33,000 Puritans immigrated to New England. They came with a vision of creating a "Holy Commonwealth"—a society based upon a covenant with God. By 1640 there were some 35 Puritan communities established in New England, each centered on a local church.

Much attention has been given in recent years to John Winthrop's 1630 sermon, "A Model of Christian Charity," especially because of the New Testament metaphor—"a city upon a hill"—that he used to describe the Puritan experiment in America. Winthrop, a layman, was the first governor of the Massachusetts Bay Colony. He used this phrase to hold his congregation accountable—pointing out that the old world would be watching them to make sure that the community they were establishing in the new world was truly godly. Winthrop's vision expressed in this sermon was that "we must delight in each other, make others' conditions our own, rejoice together, mourn together, labor and suffer together, always having before our eyes our commission and community in the work as members of the same body."

By the time Winthrop's sermon was first published over two centuries following its delivery, it was used—more accurately, misused—as a proof text for the 19th century American doctrine of Manifest Destiny. And in the late 20th century "a city upon a hill" was President Ronald Reagan's favorite metaphor to describe the United States. (He embellished the scripture a bit by adding the adjective "shining.") During the 2008 Republican Convention, "a shining city upon a hill" was said repeatedly to justify the myth of American Exceptionality.

But Governor John Winthrop can hardly be held responsible for how his sermon to a Puritan congregation in 1630 has been subsequently used. As Sarah Vowell states in her hilarious and yet very serious book *The Wordy Shipmates,* the modern assumptions of America being exceptional and chosen by God to save the world are tempered by the Puritan's sense of accountability. "The same wakefulness the individual Calvinist was to use to keep watch over his own sins Winthrop and Cotton [pastor of First Church, Boston] called for in the group at large. This humility, this fear, was what kept their delusions of grandeur in check. That's what subsequent generations lost. From New England's Puritans we inherited the idea that America is blessed and ordained by God above all nations, but lost the fear of wrath and retribution."[8]

"Puritan" has come to be a term of ridicule. H.L. Mencken, who despised Puritanism, defined it as "the haunting fear that someone, somewhere might actually be happy." But Puritans in fact were generally a happy lot, enjoyed their beer, embraced human sexuality, and took their covenant responsibilities to one another and to God with utmost seriousness. They were intellectually rigorous and were committed to an educated clergy, demonstrated by their establishment in 1636 of the first institution of higher learning in the United States, Harvard University, with its first class comprised entirely of nine theological students. As historian Jon Butler has written, "Puritans danced and sang, and on occasion they even joked."[9]

A little over three decades after Adams highlighted the Mayflower Compact, Tocqueville commented upon the importance of this legal agreement for the subsequent development of American political institutions. He observed that all later governments in the Plymouth Colony developed out of the Mayflower Compact: New Haven in 1637, Rhode Island in 1638, Connecticut in 1639, and Providence in 1640. Each government was formed by beginning with a social contract, voluntarily binding all participants in a civil body politic and submitted to everyone for their approval.[10]

By the end of the 17th century, however, the Puritan experiment to establish a holy commonwealth in New England had ended in failure. Violence toward Native Americans, suppression of dissent (most notably in the shameful story of the exile of Anne Hutchison who had challenged the male authority of church and society), and the infamous Salem witch trials are evidence of a failed social project. The breakdown of community discipline and seduction by individual economic enterprise doomed the bold undertaking. Although Winthrop's vision of "a city on a hill" with all the community "knit together in this work as one" with accountability to others beyond these shores continues to this day as a metaphor of what America might strive for, the actuality then, as now, falls far short. Nevertheless, as democracy would subsequently develop in the United States, this religious and political story of Pilgrims and Puritans has its foundational place along with stories from other faith traditions in affirming the values essential not only to who we are as Americans, but who we might yet become.

One of the most remarkable features of the colonial period is the great diversity—religious, ethnic, racial—of the population then that we tend to take for granted today as the United States has concluded yet another official census. By the time of the Boston Tea Party America was already a melting pot. Jon Butler describes what he calls "the flowering of religious diversity" in particular. "Before 1690, 90 percent of all congregations in colonial America were either Congregationalist (as in Puritan

New England) or Anglican (as in Virginia). But by 1770 this was no longer true. ... About 20 percent of all colonial congregations were Congregationalist and about 15 percent adhered to the Church of England. By 1770 Scottish and Scots-Irish Presbyterians made up 18 percent of all colonial congregations, English and Welsh Baptists about 15 percent, and Quakers, German Lutherans, and German Reformed each claimed 5 to 10 percent of the colonial congregations. Non-English congregations by then accounted for at least 25 percent of all colonial congregations, although they had been rare before 1690, and by 1770 no single religious body could claim more than 20 percent of all the colonial congregations."[11]

There was a Jewish and Catholic presence in the American colonies, albeit each of them a small minority subject to considerable discrimination by the overwhelming Protestant majority. Jews permanently settled in the colonies beginning in 1680 and by 1720 constituted two percent of New Amsterdam, later renamed New York. Maryland, originally owned by Lord Baltimore, England's most prestigious Roman Catholic nobleman, attracted English Catholics in the 17th century until major outbreaks of anti-Catholic violence closed most churches and forced priests to return to England. Catholic roots date back even further by way of Spanish conquistadores arriving from Mexico and French missionaries from Canada. Although African-American presence predates the arrival of the Pilgrims, the Black Church did not begin to grow and thrive until the 19th century.

This summary of religious diversity in the colonial period is not to imply that everyone was churched. It is difficult to determine with certainty the question of membership and activity at the end of the 18th century, but those who were on official church roles constituted only a fraction of the total population. Historians differ in their estimate of church membership at the time of the Revolutionary War, with some claiming as many as 20 percent[12] and others as few as 12 percent.[13] This is not to be misconstrued as a sign that the population was necessarily *ir*religious. The low number of members in part reflected the strictness of church standards for membership. In fact, most Americans identified with some denomination or other. And because English Congregationalists, Scottish and Scots-Irish Presbyterians, and German Baptists and Reformed—differing in church governance but similar in reliance upon Calvinist theology—constituted almost two-thirds of church members at the time of the Revolutionary War, religious assumptions about the sovereignty of God and the sinful nature of human beings were highly influential in contributing to the founding documents of the United States of America.[14] One historian, A. James Reichley, even claims that "at the time of the revolution at least 75 percent of American citizens had grown up in families espousing some form of Puritanism."[15]

When the colonies declared their independence from the British crown in 1776, what Tocqueville referred to as "the spirit of religion" was not, however, the only influence upon the events resulting in the establishment of a new sovereign nation. There was also, again drawing upon Tocqueville, "the spirit of liberty" derived primarily from a new source of philosophical values originating from Europe as a dominant source for shaping the understanding of government.

The manner in which "the spirit of liberty" came to be expressed by the Founding Fathers was influenced by the Enlightenment which in turn had been greatly influenced by the Greek philosophical tradition. Contrary to the claims of popular religion today, the authors of our nation's founding documents were not a particularly pious lot. Few belonged in any active way to a church. Fewer yet attended worship with regularity. They were steeped in the scientific and intellectual values of the Enlightenment, the mainstream of thought in 18th century

Europe affirming great confidence in human reason and a supreme faith in rational thought.

The Declaration of Independence of 1776 is a profound testimony to and reflection of Enlightenment values. Based on the philosophical theory of natural rights, it declares: *"We hold these truths to be self-evident, that all men are created equal, that they are endowed by the Creator with certain inalienable Rights, that among these are Life, Liberty and the pursuit of Happiness."* Such truth is humanly self-evident, not divinely revealed. *"That to secure these rights, governments are instituted among Men, deriving their just powers from the consent of the governed."* Power to govern comes from the people, not necessarily from God. *"That whenever any Form of Government becomes destructive of these ends, it is the Right of the People to alter or to abolish it, and to institute new Government..."* The ordering of political life—implicit in these words—is a human invention, not necessarily a divine ordinance.

Nevertheless, religious values also permeated colonial America and influenced the Founding Fathers. Benjamin Franklin proposed that the Great Seal of the United States should portray Moses with his rod lifted and the Egyptian armies drowning in the sea. Thomas Jefferson countered with a less violent image, nevertheless scriptural: the Israelites marching through the wilderness led in the daytime by God's pillar of cloud and at nighttime by a pillar of fire.[16]

As H. Richard Niebuhr reminds us, "This (Puritan) doctrine that God alone was sovereign and that therefore all human exercise of power needed to be limited became a profound influence in American life, even when its sources were forgotten."[17]

This brief review of U.S. colonial history, emphasizing the contribution of English Pilgrims and Puritans in particular, is a reminder of Tocqueville's observation that the development of democracy on these shores cannot be fully appreciated apart from the indispensable contribution of religion. Through wave upon wave of immigration over the centuries every faith tradition has impacted the continuing evolution of American democracy. Religious leaders of every Christian denomination and of every faith can tell a story of how their spiritual ancestors have left their mark in how we shape public life and discourse today. People of faith, therefore, should not be hesitant to affirm their unique contribution to the development of America's political life.

To be sure, there are other influences in addition to orthodox religious faith that have contributed to our assumptions of what constitutes good governance, such as Deism and philosophical rationalism and other Enlightenment influences. This book is *not* making the excessive and unwarranted claim of so many television preachers that the United States is a Christian country, or its slightly more generous variation that we are exclusively of the Judeo-Christian tradition. As argued in Chapter 4, democracy cannot be understood apart from its non-religious origins. Nevertheless, clergy today have no reason to be apologetic about bringing religious values into the public square. In modern-day pluralistic America, faith-based community organizing demonstrates that religion continues to be a force to be reckoned with as "the first of America's political institutions."

Chapter 7

CALVIN AND THE CONSTITUTION

"The Puritans were suspicious of power in the hands of kings, aristocrats, priests and churches; by the same token they were suspicious of power in the hands of the people."
[H. Richard Niebuhr]

If America had only its holidays to instruct us about our origins, one would be inclined to think that our sole values were liberty, freedom, and independence. The Fourth of July—Independence Day—is a national celebration of the signing of the Declaration of Independence. This bold statement declaring our intent to reject the authority of the British king and to become a sovereign people was, however, only the first of several steps leading to the establishment of the United States of America. It led to war, of course, as military force backed up claims of sovereignty from both sides of the Atlantic—or more accurately *wars,* in the plural, that were to ebb and flow for almost four decades. But it also led to a feverish effort on the part of colonial leadership to define precisely what it had in mind when it declared its independence. What was to be the governmental structure of this new nation? How would power be organized and exercised in this fledgling democracy?

It took fifteen years for this process to unfold. It was not until 1791 that the Constitution, including its first ten amendments, was adopted and a new government was clearly defined. What we ended up with in many respects was a significant departure from, or at the least a considerable restriction of, the original democratic enthusiasm of 1776. If the United States of America memorialized its beginnings in an observation of the ratification of the Constitution, a more apt name for this holiday would be *Inter*dependence Day.

Clergy easily relate to this theme of interdependence. Core religious values of all congregations affirm that freedom cannot be separated from responsibility, i.e. in response to others in community. As stated earlier (in chapter 3), Tocqueville observed that religion "struggles against the spirit of individual independence" because of its dangerous potential for undermining human community. Community organizing is seen by so many religious leaders as a good fit because, as the name itself implies, it is about building community.

As described earlier, the values that have shaped America's origins are both Greek and Hebrew, Enlightenment and Biblical. The Declaration of Independence, although peppered with general references to Providence, is primarily an Enlightenment document. But by the time we come to the tedious process of organizing the governance of this new nation in the drafting of the Constitution, it is religious assumptions about human nature that become the dominant influence. This is by no means obvious, however, since there is no explicit reference in the Constitution to God, or for that matter even to "Providence." Although this can come across as either derogatory indictment or commendatory praise, depending upon one's biases, the U.S. Constitution is, in fact, literally "a godless document."[1]

The claim that religious assumptions are a major influence in the drafting of the U.S. Constitution is based upon an examination of religious thought during the colonial period and its European sources. While theology for the most part is a silent partner in the process of structuring the governance of the newly formed United States of America, religious values are nevertheless present in a formative way. It is the theology of John Calvin in particular that is implicit in this national organizing process.

The "spirit of religion"—Tocqueville's term—helping to

shape American democracy dated back 150 years earlier in the New World and another century before that in the Old. He considered the history of the American republic, with its unique mix of religion and politics, as being largely determined by the character of its Puritan founding. "Puritanism," he observed, "was not just a religious doctrine. In several respects it coincided with the most absolute democratic and republican theories. ... Puritanism was almost as much a political theory as it was a religious doctrine."[2] The dominant theological voice informing Puritans was Calvinism. Whether it arrived on these shores in the early 17th century by way of Puritanism from England, or in the 18th century by way of the Reformed tradition of continental Europe, the intellectual and religious genius that stood behind it all was the 16th century Protestant reformer, John Calvin. At the heart of his theology was the biblical affirmation of the sovereignty of God.

If popular thought of today had been prevalent two hundred thirty years ago, the shape of the Constitution would quite likely have been very different than it turned out to be. Government is thought of negatively by many in our times as a necessary evil in which less is always better. Modern day Americans tend to place a high value on what free and independent human beings and their political and economic institutions can do if left alone, unregulated, unfettered by social restraint. But John Calvin, and subsequent generations of Calvinists—including English Puritans (Congregationalists and Baptists) and Scottish Presbyterians in colonial America—thought otherwise.[3]

Calvin considered government to be a God-given gift to enable individual human beings to band together, govern their primitive and selfish passions, and make possible a more enlightened and responsible human society. "Owing, therefore, to the vices or defects of men," he wrote, "it is safer and more tolerable when several bear rule, that they may thus mutually assist, instruct, and admonish each other, and should any one be disposed to go too far, the others are censors and masters to curb his excess." The function of government for human beings, Calvin went on to say, "is no less than that of bread, water, sun and air; indeed, its place of honor is to ensure that humanity might be maintained among all."[4]

The Calvinism that religiously shaped colonial America held a high view of government and a low view of individual human proclivities. Actually, that is putting it mildly. Left to their own devises and desires, human beings were considered by Calvin to be totally depraved. To speak of sin is not to say that people essentially are no damn good, but it is to acknowledge the dark side to human nature. This is what Reinhold Niebuhr described when he said that "there is no level of human moral or social achievement in which there is not some corruption of inordinate self-love."[5] That is why government is good and necessary. God instituted government to encourage and protect the goodness of a sinful humanity. The function of government is to humanize.

Ironically, the Enlightenment-influenced Declaration of Independence has several references to the Creator, while the Constitution, as already stated, has no explicit religious references. Nevertheless, Calvinist assumptions about human nature and governance permeate the U.S. Constitution. This religious influence is a major reason why America ended up with a form of governance that is not a pure democracy. By the time of the Constitutional Convention the original enthusiasm for democracy had faded considerably and a concern for checking the sinful excesses of individual aspirations took the upper hand.

In the struggles to define governance during the years immediately following the radical Declaration of Independence, "The Federalist Papers" authored by James Madison, Alexander Hamilton, and John Jay, first published in 1788, document the transition from the Revolution of 1776 to the Constitution of

1787 resulting in America becoming a constitutional republic. Hamilton called it a "representative democracy." In the United States of America representatives are democratically elected, and then the country is governed by its representatives.

James Madison states the theological issue underlying the Constitutional Convention. "Ambition must be made to counteract ambition. ... It may be a reflection on human nature that such devices should be necessary to control the abuses of government. *But what is government itself, but the greatest of all reflections on human nature?* If men were angels, no government would be necessary. If angels were to govern men, neither external nor internal controls on government would be necessary. In framing a government which is to be administered by men over men, the great difficulty lies in this: you must first enable the government to control the governed, and in the second place oblige it to control itself."[6]

Those people gathered in Philadelphia during that long, hot summer of 1787 were concerned about the possible excesses of democracy. They saw constitutional government as a means of channeling the otherwise destructive impulses of the unfettered democratic spirit. For that matter, it was a different group of men writing the Constitution than those who had signed the Declaration of Independence. Only six of the first group that had gathered in 1776 were present eleven years later in Philadelphia. "Leaks" from that Constitutional Convention reveal this strong desire to control the passions of individual citizens. Edmond Randolph said that the evils from which the country suffered at the time originated in "the turbulence and follies of democracy." Eldridge Gerry complained that "the evils we experience flow from the excess of democracy. The people do not want virtue, but are dupes of pretended patriots." John Adams cautioned: "Remember, democracy never lasts long. It soon wastes, exhausts, and murders itself. There never was a democracy yet that did not commit suicide." Hamilton inquired:

"Why has government been instituted at all? Because the passions of men will not conform to the dictates of reason and justice without constraint."[7]

No, these people could not be accused of believing that individuals, if left to themselves with the least government possible, would do anything other than self-destruct. As political scientist Richard Hofstadter states the issue: "The men who drew up the constitution in Philadelphia during the summer of 1787 had a vivid Calvinistic sense of human evil and damnation and believed with Hobbes that men are selfish and contentious."[8]

What finally emerged in the Constitution, culminating four years later with the ratification of the Bill of Rights, is indeed, in Madison's words, a reflection on human nature. Religious values informing an understanding of the human proclivity to abuse power informed these foundational documents. In seeking limitation by means of constitutionalism, the discussions held during the Constitutional Convention reflected Calvin's assumptions about both the possibility and necessity of government. As the theologian H. Richard Niebuhr observed, Puritans "recognized that legal power was necessary for curbing unregenerate power, and therefore agreed to civil government, but because the exercise of power tended to corrupt men, they sought limitations by means of constitutionalism, the Scriptures and 'political covenants,' and the dispersion of power."[9]

All of the above Calvinistic assumptions about government and human limitations can be found in the Constitution and the Bill of Rights: (1) constitutional guarantees of civil rights, protecting individuals from possible abuses of majority, democratic rule; (2) political agreement to govern with the consent of the governed by mutual covenant; and (3) a dispersion of power through an elaborate system of checks and balances.

The system of checks and balances, reflecting an awareness of the human tendency to abuse power, is expressed by the

Constitution in a number of ways as it describes how government is to be organized. First, a strong central government would keep a check on democratic uprisings in the various states. Under the new Constitution, "The United States shall guarantee to every State in this Union a Republican Form of Government." [Article 4, Section 4] Secondly, through representative government the actual decisions would be made one step removed from the populace. In a direct democracy the unpredictable and unstable passions of the mob could take over. Representation would provide a filtering process. Thirdly, a split congress, into Senate and Representatives, not only would placate those large states which insisted upon greater representation, but it would provide a balance between the democracy and the aristocracy—the common people choosing their representatives every two years in their own immediate districts, and the senators chosen from among notable leaders statewide for six year terms. And fourthly, independent branches of government were established, each with its own sphere of responsibility that cannot be usurped by any other branch, and with a cumbersome impeachment process designed so as to prevent one part of government from capriciously imposing its will upon another.

Values—both democratic and religious—lie at the heart of faith-based community organizing. It is what drives this form of political work. It is not power, nor self-interest, nor relationships—as important as all of these are as foundational components, but it is values that undergird and drive this particular political engagement that is faith-based community organizing.

These values, especially those arising from religious faith, embody a healthy respect for human limitation and therefore a modest assessment of what is achievable by political action. Self-governance is not free from the abuse of power—what the Bible calls "sin." There is, therefore, no ideal society on earth, no perfect political governance, no utopia capable of ordering life that fully honors the human spirit. For persons of faith it is a vision of God's reign, and not mere human rule, that is affirmed as the last word in ordering political life.

Glenn Tinder proposes the idea of "the prophetic stance" as the most appropriate political attitude for religious persons, and for Christians in particular. "The attitude it calls for is neither conservative nor revolutionary. It is not cynical; nor is it, in the usual sense of the word, idealistic. It is different even from attitudes prominently displayed by many professed Christians. It is distant, for example, from the faith that Christian standards are represented unambiguously in the free market and the bourgeois family; but it is equally distant from the idea that the political implications of the life of Christ can be adequately realized through revolution. It requires human beings to be politically serious yet forbids them to join *unreservedly* in any of the collective activities that make up the visible political life of the human race."[10]

Religious communities of faith have managed over the years to survive in every imaginable form of political governance—monarchic, capitalistic, communistic, democratic. And yet the values of democracy in the world today seem to be an especially good match for the values of biblical faith with its emphasis upon justice-love and the exaltation of the human being. As Tinder is even bold to claim, "Christianity implies democracy."[11]

In the depth of World War II, when fascism threatened to dominate the western world and communism lurked all around the edges, Reinhold Niebuhr drew upon a biblical metaphor in his vindication of democracy and critique of its traditional defense. "The children of this world are in their generation wiser than the children of light." [Luke 16:8] His central thesis was that a free society prospers best in a cultural, religious, and moral atmosphere that encourages neither a too pessimistic nor too optimistic view of human nature. The "children of darkness" (or children of this world) were defined as those who believe there is no law beyond their will and interest. The "children of light" were those who believed that self-interest should be brought under the discipline of a higher law. The children of darkness are evil, Niebuhr argued, because they know no law beyond the self. They are smart and frightfully effective, though evil. By contrast the children of light tend to underestimate the power of unrestrained and unaccountable self-interest, both individual and collective—not only as it is manifested among the children of darkness, but in their innocence of underestimating this power in themselves.[12]

Religion and politics do indeed go together in community organizing—carefully to be sure, and critically, and faithfully. Religious values and democratic values form the twin pillars that support its important work. People of faith cannot create an ideal world, but they can join with others in helping to make our world at least a bit more human. Democracy depends upon an awareness of the dark side of human nature so that the existence of power can be dealt with realistically. Likewise, democracy depends upon an appreciation of the capacity of the human spirit to transcend itself so that life with meaning and responsibility and freedom is possible. If either of these is missing, we end up with sentimentalized optimism or with cynical pessimism.

Clergy, as leaders of congregations based on religious values, have a unique perspective from which to understand modern political activity. Grounded in a knowledge of the limitation of the human spirit as well as its potential, persons engaged in faith-based community organizing discover again and again that *demokratia* is exceptionally fertile soil for the civic life. And that it presents a rare opportunity to manifest publicly, albeit in limited and fragmentary form, nothing less than what it trusts to be life as the sovereign God intends it to be. As Reinhold Niebuhr put it so succinctly in his classic phrase: "Man's capacity for justice makes democracy possible; but man's inclination to injustice makes democracy necessary."[13]

Chapter 8

A QUESTION OF PATERNITY

"We are surrounded by so great a cloud of witnesses..."
[Hebrews 12:1]

Modern community organizing in America has come a long way since its origins in the labor movement and the civil rights movement and Saul Alinsky's neighborhood-based organization in Chicago. Religious congregations have taken this approach to participating in the public arena and have adapted it to its purposes. As organizing has evolved from neighborhood-based to congregation-based and faith-based, considerable work has yet to be done in understanding this political activity from a religious perspective.

Community organizing is democracy in practice. It is not the only way to address the crisis facing our democracy, but it is one that ordinary families have access to and that gets results. Because democracy is literally "the rule of the people," enfranchisement is essential to good governance. The right to vote lies at the heart of a healthy democracy. Enfranchisement, however, is not only a matter of who gets to vote and who chooses to exercise that right. More importantly, it is about what happens between elections. That is when decisions of public policy are made by elected and appointed officials that impact upon the daily lives of citizens. Through community organizing persons feeling otherwise disconnected from their government discover what it means to be truly enfranchised.

Community organizing is the exercise of radical democracy. Saul Alinsky is often called the "father" of 20th century organizing. (One author who has written extensively about the democratic enterprise and political activism even refers to him as "the *godfather* of modern community organizing"!)[1] Alinsky asks, "what is a radical?" He then goes on to answer his own question by writing movingly of the American people. "America's radicals are to be found wherever and whenever America moves close to the fulfillment of its democratic dream. Whenever America's hearts are breaking, there American radicals were and are. America was begun by its radicals. America was built by its radicals. The hope and future of America lies with its radicals."[2]

Radical can be a scary word. It often connotes wild and crazy, attacking all that is old and precious. But in organizing it is used in its most literal sense. It means going to the root of things, to the source. (Latin *radix* = root.) Organizing is grass-roots political activity. In that sense, being radical is the ultimate conservative value. Putting democracy to work means going back to our roots by taking seriously our nation's original belief expressed in the Declaration of Independence—that "governments… derive their just powers from the consent of the governed." And because the Constitution defines America as a republic, a representative democracy, organizing goes back to the source by holding public officials accountable to the rule of the people.

For community organizing that considers itself faith-based, however, there is an appeal to "roots" that reach far deeper than the contribution made by Alinsky. The patriarchal status commonly attributed to him is challenged by religious congregations participating in organizing. In African-American culture, for example, there are many 20th century leaders who would be affirmed as being considerably more important for faith-based organizing, such as civil rights leader Ella Baker. To stay with the parental metaphor, she could be called a matriarch of modern community organizing as manifested in the civil rights movement. [3] But roots of faith-based organizing reach far deeper than our modern times. When people of faith, of whatever race or religious denomination, speak in terms of roots they look back centuries, millennia even, to claim sacred sources for an understanding of what constitutes governance that is truly radical.

However, this is not to diminish the important innovative role played by Saul Alinsky as a prime strategist of modern community organizing. He himself never claimed to have a model. Rather, he established principles, techniques, and tactics for organizing. His methodology continues to inform organizers. Stephen Hart notes how organizers tend not to learn their craft in school or from books, but by being trained by organizers from the previous generation—"a kind of apostolic succession" that almost always leads back to Alinsky.[4]

Saul Alinsky developed the fundamental concepts and methodology of organizing in the late 1930s through his earliest and most important project, the Back of the Yards Neighborhood Council in Chicago. Key components include: 1) Values of democracy as the grounding of community organizing; 2) Self-interest as the starting point for any social change; 3) Power analysis—external as well as internal—to understand how decisions are made; 4) Relationship building through active listening on a one-to-one basis; 5) Leadership development of ordinary persons committed to doing the work; 6) Accountability to one another in the organization and to the families of the community, as well as holding elected and appointed officials accountable for their public trust. 7) Actions (organized and highly disciplined mass meetings) to put political pressure on officials to respond to the interests of ordinary families participating in this political process.

Jewish by birth, Alinsky was not religiously observant. Although secular in his orientation, Alinsky "continually used language that bespoke a transcendent commitment to the ideal of democracy, speaking of 'sacred values' and 'our democratic faith.'"[5] It could be said that his religion was democracy itself.

He worked with religious leaders and churches, along with other community institutions, as important for mobilizing power, but understood their faith and values as strictly internal matters unrelated to the organizing effort. Mark Warren notes that Alinsky was not particularly interested in the cultures and belief systems of the churches he recruited. He reports a later recollection by a Catholic pastor who had worked closely with Alinsky. When Fr. John Egan advocated more discussion of religious values within the Back of the Yards Neighborhood Council, Alinsky responded, "You take care of the religion, Jack, we'll do the organizing."[6]

Since Alinsky's death in 1972 most of the major community organizing networks—including Industrial Areas Foundation (IAF), PICO National Network, The Gamaliel Foundation, Direct Action Research & Training (DART)—have evolved into organizations that take seriously, along with the secular values of democracy, values that are derived from the history of religious faith traditions. Whether they refer to themselves as faith-based or congregation-based or broad-based, these community organizing networks all understand their political activity to be informed by the culture and belief-systems of the participating institutions.

So, how do we speak of the religious roots of faith-based community organizing? Without taking anything away from Alinsky's indispensable role as an innovative strategist and tactician, another metaphor is required than the usual one attributing fatherhood to him. Where do we turn to discover additional sources to account for and to clarify the religious parentage of organizing that is faith-based?

The Letter to the Hebrews speaks of being "surrounded by so great a cloud of witnesses..." [12:1] In the prior chapter of this New Testament book the author credentials a definition of faith—"the assurance of things hoped for, the conviction of things not seen"—by appealing to the generations that had gone before, naming ancestors of the faith reaching back as far as the original biblical family of Adam and Eve. This line of argumentation is truly radical in the sense of going to the roots. Departing from the usual practice of naming a single "father" of community organizing, this book considers instead a multitude of ancestors as a more appropriate way to describe organizing that is grounded in the life of religious congregations. In this chapter and the next we stay with the family metaphor by considering the witness of four religious forebears of modern, faith-based community organizing.

The Social Gospel Movement: "Kingdom of God"

The witness of mainline Protestantism is the ancestor this writer is most intimately acquainted with through having been a lifelong member of the United Church of Christ and, before it came into being in 1957, one of its predecessor denominations, the Congregational-Christian Churches. So-called "mainline" churches have many theological sources, some of which have been discussed earlier. One relatively recent source in particular that is worthy of emphasis is the Social Gospel movement. In the last decade of the 19th century and the beginning of the 20th century Walter Rauschenbusch developed a theology that affirmed the social dimension to life. Although socially and religiously conservative as a German Baptist living in New York City, he prophetically railed against the exploitation of the common person by industry and government, and he took the church to task for its silent collusion with the powers-that-be. He issued a call for the church to become engaged in politics. Participation in the democratic process was a religious imperative deriving from Jesus who "democratized the conception of God."[7]

Rauschenbusch, as H. Richard Niebuhr has observed, was a child of 19th century Protestant evangelicalism. The dawning of the 20th century demonstrated the inadequacy of this theology for the new situation that had developed. Evangelicalism, greatly influenced by Enlightenment notions of individualism, "could not emancipate itself from the conviction—more true in its time than in ours—that the human unit is the individual. It was unable therefore to deal with social crisis, with national disease and the misery of human groups." Evangelicalism continued to think of crisis in private terms of individual death. Seeds of a new paradigm were present, however, as it began to think of promise in social terms.[8]

Writing in critical response to a Christianity that had become excessively private and individualistic, Rauschenbusch interpreted the biblical faith tradition—the prophets of the Old Testament as well as Jesus and Paul of the New Testament—as expressing a commitment to social justice. Without renouncing his evangelical origins, he adapted his belief in Jesus' cross and resurrection, and human redemption and atonement, by affirming divine sovereignty. He took the Kingdom of God—a metaphor that is both religious and political—as expressing the essence of the social gospel. "The Kingdom of God is humanity organized according to the will of God."[9]

Sin is not only personal, Rauschenbusch argued, it is also social. "Sin is not a private transaction between the sinner and God. Humanity always crowds the audience room when God holds court. We must democratize the conception of God; then the definition of sin will become more realistic." The social gospel did not take away individual responsibility, but shifted the emphasis by assigning a new valuation to different classes of sins. "Those who do their thinking in the light of the Kingdom of God make less of heresy and private sins," reserving their righteous indignation for the myriad of injustices that are the truly unforgivable sins.[10]

Likewise, salvation is social as well as personal. "Complete salvation, therefore, would consist in an attitude of love in which he would freely coordinate his life with the life of his fellows in obedience to the loving impulses of the spirit of God, thus taking his part in a divine organism of mutual service." [11] This divine organism is the public sphere. Religion is best practiced not in private, but in public. Human community becomes the arena where the life of faith must be lived.

The Social Gospel has its limitations and is not without its critics. As the 20th century unfolded, its influential role in shaping the political understanding of faith for American Protestants took a back seat to succeeding theologies—such as Neo-Orthodoxy, Christian Realism, Liberation (Political) Theology, Black Theology, Feminism, Biblical Theology in Political/Cultural Context, and so on.

Nevertheless, the Social Gospel, by shifting Protestantism from a one-sided emphasis upon the private to a concern for the public realm, deserves to be named as one of the ancestors of faith-based community organizing. Although exponents of this social gospel at times risked the error of believing that the reign of God could be fully institutionalized—that the divine will could totally be identified with a particular social program—the greater witness for which it is remembered today is the shift of emphasis from the private to the public, from the isolated individual to the human community. As Niebuhr said, "The kingdom of God in America is neither an ideal nor an organization. It is a movement which, like the city of God described by Augustine in ancient times, appears in only partial and mixed manner in the ideas and institutions in which men seek to fix it."[12]

Catholic Social Teachings: "The Common Good"

Another ancestor of faith-based community organizing is Catholic social teaching. Thanks to the Second Vatican Council and the ecumenical movement of the mid-20th century, there has been considerable interaction between Protestants and Catholics. In no setting has this ecumenical relationship been stronger than in faith-based community organizing. Of all the interdenominational groups this writer has participated in over the years of being a pastor—local councils of churches, ecumenical councils, ministerial associations—it is community organizing more than anything else that has provided the context for serious theological discussion, effective political activity, and the development of strong relationships with both clergy and laity.

Modern Catholic social teaching was birthed in the late 19th century at approximately the same time as the Social Gospel. Jesuit John Coleman prefers the term "social Catholicism," acknowledging not only official teachings but the broad spectrum of theological thought shaping modern Catholic ethics. He argues that there are many sources influencing the Catholic approach to relating the faith to the public sphere, such as liberation theology and the base communities in the Latin American Church, the rise of Solidarity in Poland, Pax Christi, the Catholic Worker Movement, to name a few.[13]

But it is the Catholic Social Teachings found in papal encyclicals and apostolic letters, the declaration and the pastoral constitution by the Second Vatican Council, and two pastoral letters from the U.S. Catholic Bishops that constitute the body of documents under consideration here as one of the "ancestors" of community organizing.

Although there is no official canon, or listing, of what in particular constitutes modern Catholic Social Teachings, there is nevertheless a general consensus that some fifteen ecclesiastical documents are included, beginning in 1891 with the encyclical *Rerum novarum* (The Condition of Labor) by Pope Leo XIII. These address a range of modern concerns: political and economic issues prompted by the Industrial Revolution, condemnation of the extremes of socialism and capitalism, rights of workers and the social dimension of private property, human rights and religious freedom, dignity of the human person and the essential importance of human community, economic development to address the growing gap between rich and poor, the challenge of peace and of economic justice.[14]

The concepts articulated in these official teachings and the larger body of Catholic ethical thinking over the past century—what Coleman refers to as social Catholicism—are fundamentally in agreement. "The four essential marks of sound Catholic social thought—distributive justice and the notions of solidarity, human dignity, subsidiarity, the preferential option for the poor—are ultimately connected and linked and indeed cannot be understood independently of each other."[15]

In 1971 the international synod of bishops (the Roman Synod) published a document on justice, *Justitia in mundo* (Justice in the World), that emphasized the mission of the church as being concerned not simply with the conversion of private souls but with the social transformation of the world. In it is found what is perhaps the most commonly quoted sentence from all the official documents, expressing in spirit and essence the totality of modern Catholic Social Teachings. "Action on behalf of justice and participation in the transformation of the world fully appear to us as a constitutive dimension of the preaching of the Gospel."[16]

It is a characteristic of Catholic teaching to emphasize continuity with the past and to downplay new developments. Nevertheless, the Second Vatican Council represented a significant departure from earlier understandings of the relationship between the church and world. Triumphalism was replaced with the concept of the pilgrim church. Private faith and public witness of the laity were affirmed as inseparable. The central role of Scripture in the church was restored. And, of special importance to the topic at hand, democracy was embraced. The Catholic Church in the 19th century opposed democracy, but by the end of the 20th century it had become a leader in advocating the cause of democracy throughout the entire world.[17]

Fundamental to Catholic teaching is the belief, articulated by Thomas Aquinas in the 13th century, that the human being is social and political by nature. Correspondingly, government is affirmed as a gift of God. The State is understood to be natural, necessary, and good. It is limited in its authority. And its purpose is the Common Good.[18]

Solidarity, human dignity, subsidiarity (local control), and a preferential option for the poor are all linked in the concept of the Common Good. When Pope John Paul II made solidarity a central theme in his social teaching he was not only showing the influence of the Solidarity movement in his native Poland, but used it in a much broader sense. "When interdependence becomes recognized in this way, the correlative response as a moral and social attitude, as a 'virtue,' is solidarity. This then is not a feeling of vague compassion or shallow distress at the misfortunes of so many people, both near and far. On the contrary, it is a firm and persevering determination to commit oneself to the common good; that is to say to the good of all and of each individual because we are all really responsible for all."[19]

The modern Catholic concept of the Common Good opens the way for the church to work in partnership with others in a pluralistic democratic society—not only with other religious institutions, but with labor, capital, government, etc. The Common Good pushes beyond the limited and distorted view of radical individualism in which competing interest groups simply broker their demands. It leads to an actual mutual deliberation.[20]

Pope Benedict XVI drew upon the concept of the Common Good in his 2007 Holy Week message to the church: "Worship pleasing to God can never be a purely private matter, without consequences for our relationships with others; it demands a public witness to our faith, the promotion of the common good in all its forms." [*Sacramentum caritatis,* "Sacrament of Charity"]

This emphasis upon the Common Good continues to be a hallmark of the Catholic Church in these opening years of the 21st century. As recently as September 17, 2010, Pope Benedict addressed a concern for the marginalization of religion. The venue was significant. This was the first time ever a pontiff had spoken in Westminster Hall. Pope Benedict praised Britain as a pluralistic society valuing freedom of speech and of political affiliation, arguing forcefully for "the legitimate role of religion in the public square."

+ + + + +

Up to this point we have considered two "ancestors" of faith-based community organizing. In the next chapter we will continue to explore branches on the family tree by looking at two more faith traditions as sources of religious values.

Chapter 9

MORE BRANCHES ON THE FAMILY TREE

"And because he loved your ancestors, he chose their descendants after them. He brought you out of Egypt with his own presence, by his great power..."
[Deuteronomy 4:37]

Continuing with the family metaphor we come to two more ancestors of modern faith-based community organizing—Judaism and the African-American Church. Beginning with the former, it has been this writer's experience, both with respect to interpreting the scriptures as well as approaching social issues, that at many points one can have far more in common with Jews than with some Christians. This is not everyone's experience, to be sure. Nevertheless, for this writer, it is community organizing more than any other setting that provides a constructive context for serious interfaith conversation and action.

Tikkun olam: "Repairing the World"

The title of an introductory article by Rabbi Jonah Pesner, Founding Director of *Just Congregations* (of the Union for Reform Judaism), on the theme of community organizing in the journal *Sh'ma,* asks: "Will Synagogues Organize for Justice?" There is no question of the commitment to justice that lies at the heart of the Jewish religion. But Pesner is challenging synagogues and temples to consider community organizing as a method for doing justice. He writes of congregation-based organizing as "the revolutionary way in which the Jewish community is pursuing justice." A synagogue-sponsored "action" ended with the leader, in his role as host, congratulating "the hundreds of temple members for honoring their deeply held Jewish values by holding their elected leaders accountable to principles of social justice."[1]

One of the several contributions of Judaism to community organizing is an appreciation of diversity. Jonathan Sacks, Chief Rabbi of the United Hebrew Congregations of Britain and the Commonwealth, reflects upon Judaism's foundational affirmation of "the dignity of difference." He locates the celebration of diversity at the very heart of the monotheistic imagination. The book of Genesis "was the first to see all humankind as bound by a universal covenant, and yet to acknowledge the legitimacy of profound religious and cultural differences." The biblical concept of covenant affirms the dignity of difference. Because covenants are relational, they are inherently pluralistic. "Fundamentalism, like imperialism, is the attempt to impose a single truth on a plural world. It is the Tower of Babel of our time. ... The test of faith is whether I can make space for difference."[2]

The value placed here upon the uniqueness of each religious tradition, identifying difference as a source of strength, lies at the heart of faith-based community organizing. The organizing work of each congregation is driven by its own values. Organizing provides a context for religious congregations of diverse traditions and theologies to come together around shared concerns for the larger community, respecting the particular values that drive each of the participants and in the process discerning common values for public life.

One of the points of difference refers to the word "faith" itself. Christians commonly speak of their religious experience in terms of faith, as something one *has*, while Jews tend to speak more of religion as something one *does*. Even the language of being "faith-based," therefore, can be something of an issue. The term "faith" is commonly used in America today as a synonym for religion. And in our culture religion is oftentimes understood primarily as a private affair. According to this popular usage, the term "faith-based" is subject to a distorted understanding of being private and individualistic. But Jews, when speaking of the topic under consideration, tend to refer to "congregation-based" community organizing. The term is technically correct and speaks more clearly of the fundamental characteristic that marks the approach to organizing discussed in this book. The faith-based organizing model implies participation in a religious community. When a person states his or her credentials in a one-to-one or in an action, the congregation that one belongs to or in some way affiliates with is included. In other words, as Jewish terminology correctly emphasizes, we are speaking here of organizing that is congregation-based.

A third point of emphasis with respect to understanding the role of religion in the public sphere is an emphatic witness to what Thomas Jefferson called "the wall of separation" between church and state. To be sure, for the most part in America today Catholics and Protestants likewise affirm the importance of a separation of state power from the power of religious institutions. (It has not always been this way. In this writer's own faith tradition, Congregationalism was the legally established religion in the State of Connecticut until 1834, over four decades following the ratification of the United States Constitution and the First Amendment.) Born of the experience of being a minority in Christendom for most of two millennia, and bearing the scars of coercive abuse and violent persecution, Jews tend to be especially sensitive to maintaining boundaries between church and state. In no way is this understood as a privatization of religion. Jews, as well as Catholics and Protestants, affirm that religious values must be brought to bear on public issues. But Jews help all of us to remember that no particular religious tradition has the exclusive right to impose its agenda upon the nation at large, any more than government can legitimately use its power to favor a particular religion.

Judaism is abundantly rich with the Torah and Prophets of sacred scripture, rabbinic teachings and arguments of the Talmud, mystical traditions of the Kaballah, prayer and ritual and theological reflection. All of this is grist for the mill for rabbis and leaders in synagogues and temples reflecting upon values that inform their political activity through congregation-based community organizing. Most central of all is the story of the Exodus, the formative narrative for the people of God in the Hebrew Scriptures. It is a story that has also been a key metaphor for Puritanism in the colonial period, for liberation theology for Catholics and Protestants in the 20th century, and especially for African-American church experience.

Michael Walzer identifies the story of the Exodus as a paradigm for what he calls "revolutionary politics." In the society at large this has been the characteristic way of thinking about political change since late medieval or early modern times. "So pharaonic oppression, deliverance, Sinai, and Canaan are still with us, powerful memories shaping our perceptions of the political world. ... We still believe, or many of us do, what the Exodus first taught, or what it has commonly been taken to teach, about the meaning and possibility of politics and about its proper form: first, that wherever you live, it is probably Egypt; second, that there is a better place, a world more attractive, a promised land; and third, that 'the way to the land is through the wilderness.' There is no way to get from here to there except by joining together and marching."[3]

Finally, a Jewish concept that has captured the moral and political imagination of Jews for centuries, and relatively recently has powerfully spoken to Christians and others as well, is: *Tikkun olam*. It is translated as mending, or healing, or repairing, or perfecting the world. This idea is ancient in origin, the phrase appearing in one of Judaism's best-known prayers, *Alenu,* said at the end of each of the daily services. The paragraph in which it appears, as Sacks points out, is one of the great universalistic statements of the prayer book. "It is our hope, O Lord our God, ...to perfect the world [*le-takken olam*] under the sovereignty of the Almighty..."[4]

Tikkun olam has come to be virtually synonymous with social justice. Yet it is far more than that, certainly more than any particular political agenda. It is a spiritual reality in which a person prayerfully partners with God in being a co-creator of the world. The broken/fractured world is mended/repaired in small steps. On one hand, redemption comes from God. On the other hand, without human participation there is nothing through which God can act. *Tikkun olam* is "a redemption of small steps, act by act, day by day." Far more than a matter of law, justice in the Hebrew Bible is the act of restoring a broken order.[5]

Sacks concludes his thoughts on *Tikkun olam,* in a manner typical of much Jewish reflection, by telling an ancient story and then commenting upon it. "Hassidim tell the story of the second Lubavitcher Rebbe (the 'Mitteler' Rebbe) who was once so intent on his studies that he failed to hear the cry of his baby son. His father (Rebbe Shneur Salman of Ladi) heard, and went down and took the baby in his arms until he went to sleep again. Then he went into his son, still intent on his books, and said, 'My son, I do not know what you are studying, but it is not the study of Torah if it makes you deaf to the cry of a child.'"

This story of two generations of distinguished rabbis carries a powerful message to all leaders, perhaps especially to religious leaders. Clergy can become so consumed in doing important work, such as the political activity of helping to create a better and more human community, that perspective can be lost in the process. As Sacks comments upon the Hasidic story, "To live the life of faith is to hear the silent cry of the afflicted, the lonely and marginal, the poor, the sick and the disempowered, and to respond. For the world is not yet mended, there is work still to do, and God has empowered us to do it—with him, for him and for his faith in us."[6]

Black Theology and the Civil Rights Movement: "The Light of Freedom"

The fourth ancestor of faith-based community organizing under consideration—African-American Christianity—should be easy for a Protestant to write about. After all, Black and White churches generally share the common designation of Protestant. We read much of the same theology. Biblical preaching is central to worship. Many of us are educated in the same seminaries.

And yet, as a White guy, this writer finds the African-American ancestor to be the most difficult of all to describe—even more so than Catholic and Jewish. The reason for this is the huge racial divide that exists in our country. Racism has been called America's original sin, and for good theological reason. The doctrine of sin in Christianity speaks of a separation of life as it actually is from what God has created it to be. This rupture reaches to the root of existence. To speak of sin is to acknowledge the social dimension to life—that inter-connectedness is stained by brokenness. And it is to acknowledge that this brokenness reaches back to the beginning. The sin of racism is literally original to the American story.

James Cone, in his 1969 groundbreaking theological study, *Black Theology and Black Power,* writes of the disenchantment of Blacks with democracy—not the theoretical idea of democracy as such, but as it has been experienced as "white democracy." Near the beginning of the book, he quotes the poet Langston Hughes as articulating what the black man feels in a white world: "I swear to the Lord / I still can't see / Why Democracy means / Everybody but me."[7]

In 1619, one year before the Pilgrims landed on Plymouth Rock, the first boatload of Blacks arrived in Jamestown and were immediately sold and traded. The roots of slavery in America precede the story of The First Thanksgiving. Racism—

manifested both in the genocidal treatment of Native Americans and the institution of enslaving Africans—is an original American story. As with sin in any form, racism does not simply fade away with the passage of time—even with the Emancipation Proclamation of 1863 and the Civil Rights Act of 1964, or for that matter with the election of the first African-American president in 2008. Given a national story of origins that includes the grossly unjust legacy of buying and owning and selling human beings, it surely is not surprising that 21st century American society continues to be haunted by racial conflict.

It is not easy for African-Americans and Anglo-Americans to work together. White guilt and Black anger, both generally covert rather than overt, can derail the best of intentions to address community issues in partnership. When power has been so flagrantly abused generation after generation, it can be exceptionally challenging even to talk about power, let alone to build a powerful organization able to act to bring change to the larger community.

However, the context of faith-based community organizing can provide a safe and constructive place for conversation and action. Just as close collegial relationships among Catholics and Jews and Protestants can arise through faith-based organizing, more so than in any other ecumenical or interfaith setting, the same experience takes place between Blacks and Whites. The strongest relationships this writer has developed with Black clergy and laity have been through faith-based community organizing. By listening hard and focusing upon shared values, people learn to trust one another—not so much by talking abstractly about racism or by ideologically dwelling upon historical grievances, but by working together to create a more human community.

The African-American Church was born in slavery. Biblical stories were first learned from white oppressors interested in domesticating and controlling their slave property. The power of myth, however, is that it speaks of a reality greater than the historical vessel that holds it. The Easter story of death and resurrection, with the parallel Exodus story of slavery and liberation, was claimed by the Black Church as its own narrative of deliverance. The sacred story born of slavery was turned in upon itself, providing support to Blacks in questioning their status as slaves while at the same time becoming a means of questioning the religion of the slaveholder. The original theology of accommodation was transformed into a theology of liberation. Christianity became a powerful spiritual source expressed through song and story that continues to sustain Blacks through the most challenging of times. Far more than a mere metaphor of the spiritual life, therefore, the Exodus story of liberation from slavery is literally the story of the African-American Church.

"Black theology," Cone writes, "is as old as when the first African refused to accept slavery as consistent with religion and as recent as when a black person intuitively recognizes that the confession of the Christian faith receives its meaning only in relation to political justice."[8] This commitment of the African-American Church to the struggle for justice is one of the key religious sources driving faith-based community organizing today.

Cone's development of Black Power as a theological concept was not greeted with enthusiasm, to say the least, when he first introduced his thoughts immediately following the height of the civil rights movement. "Christianity is not alien to Black Power; it is Black Power."[9] Such talk of changing the structures of power was seen, not unexpectedly, as threatening to Whites. But this was also unsettling to many Blacks as well. Especially disconcerting was the tension that had developed earlier among civil rights leaders over the controversial publicity swirling around the unfounded accusations of Black Power equaling Black Supremacy. The media, always on the lookout for a story of dissension, suggested divisive splits among the leadership. (The same controversy continues over four decades later with spurious charges of "reverse discrimination.") But Stokely Carmichael, head of the Student Nonviolent Coordinating Committee (SNCC), while reflecting later in his autobiography, emphatically denied the rift between him and Martin Luther King Jr., head of the Southern Christian Leadership Conference. "Dr. King ... never repudiated Black Power. Never. Despite pressure, even from his own staff, he never yielded to the hysteria. ... That's a myth that he attacked us. ... The most he ever said was that the language was 'unfortunate,' being subject to 'misunderstanding by our white brothers and sisters.'"[10]

As Cone points out on theological grounds, power is not in opposition to non-violence and love. It is essential to the religious life. "Black people now know that freedom is not a gift from white society, but is, rather, the self-affirmation of one's existence as a person, a person with certain innate rights to say No and Yes, despite the consequences."[11] As community organizers affirm, power—the ability to act—is never given, only taken.

The civil rights movement itself was essentially a work of community organizing that was primarily driven by the values of African-American Christianity. We tend to interpret history as the product of solitary heroes, such as Martin Luther King Jr. and Rosa Parks. But, as Charles Payne points out, the most significant work was done over several decades by countless persons engaged in a community organizing process. The civil rights movement was defined in fact by "the developmental perspective, an emphasis on building relationships, respect for collective leadership, for bottom-up change, the expansive sense of how democracy ought to operate in everyday life, the emphasis on building for the long haul, the anti-bureaucratic ethos, the preference for addressing local issues."[12]

As important as a "win" is in community organizing, more

important is the development of leadership and the experience of being part of a powerful organization. In the organizing process itself there is a sense of growing power among all who participate. CORE's James Farmer spoke of the need "to involve the people themselves, individually, personally in the struggle for their own freedom. Not simply because it was clear that no one else was going to confer liberty upon them, but because in the very act of working for the impersonal cause of racial freedom, a man experiences, almost like grace, a large measure of private freedom. Or call it a new comprehension of his own identity, an intuition of the expanding boundaries of his self, which, if not the same thing as freedom, is its radical source."[13]

One of the most powerful civil rights leaders was Ella Baker. A gifted grassroots organizer, she devoted her entire life to civil rights. Future leaders such as Stokely Carmichael, Rosa Parks and Bob Moses were mentored by her. She served on staff of the NAACP, helped to organize the Southern Christian Leadership Conference (SCLC), and helped to found the Student Nonviolent Coordinating Committee (SNCC). She cofounded and directed the Mississippi Freedom Democratic Party that took on the national Democratic Party during the 1964 convention. Ella Baker pushed the idea of participatory democracy and was committed to action from below as opposed to top-down hierarchical movements dependent upon a charismatic leader. "The Negro must quit looking for a savior and work to save itself," she said. As Barbara Ransby has written, "Baker's unfaltering confidence in the common people was the bedrock of her political vision. It was with them that she felt the locus of power should reside."[14]

There is a technical difference between a social movement and community organizing. Both are manifested in what is commonly called the civil rights movement. Martin Luther King Jr. is well known as the most prominent face and voice to this social movement. By contrast, outside of the African-American community Ella Baker is relatively unknown. Like Dr. King, she too was a key civil rights leader. But she was devoted to a grass-roots strategy of community organizing—conducting one-to-ones, listening to ordinary people, building relationships, developing local leaders. Not surprisingly, there was tension between these two leaders. Perhaps it is apocryphal, but Baker is credited with saying: "Martin didn't make the movement; the movement made Martin." Whether actually stated in so many words or not, there is a degree of truth here that does not take anything away from Dr. King. In community organizing there is always the awareness that charismatic leaders do not make the organization, but the organization makes ordinary people into leaders.

Leaders are those who, day in, day out, do the work—knocking on doors and signing people up to vote, training new leaders in disciplines of listening and recruiting, engaging in power-analysis to discern how change can be brought about, building networks of allies, pulling large groups of people together at the strategic time to make a public statement and to bring pressure to bear upon those in positions of political authority. This is what constituted the essence of the civil rights movement. Like Ella Baker, Rosa Parks was a trained organizer. Her decision to remain in her seat on that fateful day did not come out of the blue. It had all been planned as part of an organizing strategy. As Payne says, "The popular conception of Montgomery—a tired woman refused to give up her seat and a prophet rose up to lead the grateful masses—is a good story but useless history."[15]

Payne spells out how the civil rights movement lost much of its original momentum following the great successes of the 1960s. The reason he gives is that attention was no longer given to the grassroots community organizing work that over decades had built the foundation of the civil rights movement. The legacy was not lost. Many carried the organizing philosophy with them as they moved into other arenas. Although in the years to follow many activists worked within the organizing tradition, far more came to use only the tradition's rhetoric. "It is still fair to say that the organizing tradition as a political and intellectual legacy of Black activists has been effectively lost, pushed away from the table by more top-down models."[16]

Andrew Young, colleague of Martin Luther King Jr. and subsequently U.S. Ambassador to the United Nations, Mayor of Atlanta, and an ordained minister of the United Church of Christ, reflected upon developments in the past four decades for a video project conducted by the PICO National Network. He draws a parallel between the civil rights movement of the 1960s and faith-based community organizing of today. "When you hear people all over the world saying 'we shall overcome' ... that inspiration came from, really, fourteen churches, and a small group of people, in a southern city that most people had never heard of. Most people had never heard of Martin Luther King before the March on Washington. And Birmingham was before the March on Washington. The world has changed so drastically in the last forty years. ... Nothing about me, or Martin Luther King, was particularly exceptional. It was interesting that one of the college presidents who interviewed Martin for a job as chaplain didn't offer it to him because he questioned his leadership ability. They figured he was not a strong enough leader to lead college students. And so he went to Montgomery. I don't think all of these things are accidental. Coincidence is God's way of remaining anonymous. It's my belief that there is a divine spirit, a Holy Spirit, that's moving in and among the affairs of men and of nations, and we think of that as the coming of the Kingdom. And I think that when you look at PICO organizers that's essentially what they're doing. They are mobilizing deeds of love and mercy to make our communities and our nation more like the Kingdom of God."[17]

Race continues to be an issue in American politics. When candidate Barack Obama's campaign threatened to be derailed by his close association with his United Church of Christ pastor, who had become a political liability, he stood across the street from Constitution Hall in Philadelphia and addressed the American people in what will surely endure as one of the most insightful and powerful speeches ever on the topic of race. He spoke openly and directly of that which has been virtually taboo in political campaign discourse. The U.S. Constitution that gloriously calls for "a more perfect union" is also a document shamefully "stained by the nation's original sin of slavery." This legacy need not be perpetuated forever, he argued. "We have a choice in this country. We can accept a politics that breeds division, and conflict, and cynicism. ... Or, we can come together and say, 'Not this time.'" As never before in such a public setting and to such a huge audience, Obama spoke of race as "an issue I believe this nation cannot afford to ignore right now." The promises of the American Dream that so many have worked so hard to achieve have been denied to the "many who didn't make it—those who were ultimately defeated, in one way or the other, by discrimination." Obama appealed to the higher values of the American people by challenging everyone to work together to accomplish the Constitution's ideal of becoming "a more perfect union."

This powerful speech turned Barack Obama's campaign around and helped to get him elected. But it hardly marked the end of racial politics in America. What has changed, if anything, is that the issue is more out in the open than before. As Cornel West observed 15 years earlier, democracy is still at risk. "We are living in one of the most frightening moments in the history of this country. ... Every historic effort to forge a democratic project has been undermined by two fundamental realities: *poverty* and *paranoia*. ... Race is the most explosive issue in American life precisely because it forces us to confront the tragic facts of poverty and paranoia, despair and mistrust. In short, a candid examination of *race* matters takes us to the core of the crisis of American democracy. And the degree to which race *matters* in the plight and predicament of fellow citizens is a crucial measure of whether we can keep alive the best of this democratic experiment we call America."[18]

+ + + + +

There is no need to stop with only four ancestors as religious sources informing faith-based community organizing. Another family member that could be considered is the Farm Worker Movement in which Cesar Chavez built a labor union based upon a diverse set of values—Roman Catholic religious heritage, Hispanic culture, a militantly non-violent strategy influenced by Mahatma Gandhi and Martin Luther King, Jr., and the organizing skills of his teacher, Saul Alinsky.

Unitarian-Universalists, with their longstanding witness to social justice, are an important part of the organizing family. Likewise, Quakers (Society of Friends) and Mennonites have long taken the lead in giving voice to those who otherwise have too easily been pushed to the margins and thereby ignored.

The family of faith-based community organizing is wide open. All who are willing to work with those of other faith traditions, at the point where they determine their self-interests to be shared, are potential organizing partners. There could also be Mormon members of the family. And Buddhist. And, as is beginning to happen in some organizing projects, there are Muslim members as well.

The point is that the faith-based organizing family is made up of any congregation that chooses to participate. There is no creedal or ideological test for membership. Being "faith-based" does not imply sharing the same religious faith. What *is* shared is a willingness to work together to build community in the public sphere. This community is based upon democratic values shared by all Americans. In addition and most importantly, each congregation brings to the organizing effort its own particular set of religious values that shape its life.

The seminal contribution of Saul Alinsky for all modern community organizing is not in question. But the largely secular model he originated is obviously lacking at several points when religious congregations choose to engage in political activity. The basic concepts of community organizing introduced by Alinsky are still affirmed, but with significant redefinition. For people of faith, individual self-interest cannot be considered apart from a commitment to a community of self-interest. Power—the ability to act—is as central for congregations as it was for Alinsky, but it is theologically nuanced in terms of justice-love rather than of coercive force. Relationships are key to all political work, but religious expression is more at home with a relational model than with a confrontational model. And values—godly values that constitute the heartbeat of ministry and mission—are obviously central as the driving force of faith-based organizing.

Faith-based organizing has powerful religious roots as diverse as the many congregations that participate. Diversity is affirmed not as an ideological abstraction, but as a powerful reality. As with any family, each member has an essential role to play. Because faith-based organizing is driven by values and not by issues, the unique gifts and perspectives of each congregation are celebrated as central to the shared work of strengthening the larger community.

The roots of this approach to community organizing grow deep in the conviction that faith is "the assurance of things hoped for, the conviction of things not seen." [Hebrews 11:1] Results are important, of course, in any attempt to create a more human community. But hope is prior. It is the belief that God is an ally in the process that gives this particular work its driving power. To believe in God is to trust that the future is open. The spiritual ancestors live on in the present life of communities of faith through their ministry and mission. It is nothing less than a great cloud of witnesses surrounding faith-based community organizing that sustains and guides the challenging work of building radical democracy in our own times.

Introduction to Part II

THE ORGANIZING FORCE FIELD: PERSONAL REFLECTIONS UPON FOUNDATIONAL CONCEPTS

The second section of this book is more personal in nature and therefore is written in the first-person. These reflections on the foundational concepts of faith-based community organizing arise from the author's experience in serving a congregation. I have always been a pastor, never a professional organizer. But as I learned about the organizing process and put it into practice in the congregation, I came to consider myself an organizing pastor.

A word about terminology is in order at this point. Faith traditions employ a variety of terms to refer to the congregational office of religious leader—pastor, rabbi, imam, minister, reverend, father, sister, deacon, elder, etc. Some Protestant congregations are headed by a bishop. The most inclusive term might be "authorized religious leader." Although accurate, this feels awkward. The term used throughout this book—pastor—reflects the author's faith tradition as well as that of many others. Its usage here is intended to refer inclusively to all who are authorized by their respective ecclesiastical governing bodies to provide religious leadership to a congregation.

The particular reference to "organizing pastor" is also intentional. Some speak of the "pastor as organizer" to refer to the religious leader of a congregation participating in faith-based community organizing. In my opinion, this phrase puts the emphasis in the wrong place. For the religious leader and the congregation, it is the pastoral role, not organizing, that is central. Although subtle, to speak of an "organizing *pastor*" places the emphasis where it belongs—upon the clergy office.

The best theology for the pastor—certainly the most useful, in my opinion—is reflection upon the daily practice of ministry. What I learned in the seminary classroom was invaluable in providing a foundation for everything to follow. But it was after I was ordained and was working in the church that theology came alive for me. No longer an abstraction, it became vividly concrete and intensely personal. Theological reflection was not an optional activity in my busy life as a pastor, but I discovered it to be the practical tool that made sense of and gave direction to everything I was doing—not only the obvious task of preparing the weekly sermon, but in the mundane business of running a church, such as developing a budget and overseeing staff. Theology for me became an essential part of my pastoral survival kit.

Being actively involved in community organizing only heightened this awareness. It was clearly my job, as a pastor, to reflect theologically on the organizing work of the congregation. Without theological reflection there would be no spiritual roots to ensure that this political activity was consistent with the purposes of the church.

And there is something about organizing itself that encourages reflection on what is actually happening. There is little patience for what too often passes as church business—

sitting around and discussing endlessly and talking something to death. While faith-based community organizing is value-driven, it is also action-oriented. Instead of engaging in "armchair theology" unrelated to a specific context, organizing encourages what I think of as "on the job theology." By its very practical nature of staying focused on getting the work done, organizing has little use for the kind of theology that, to borrow from Johnny Cash, is so heavenly minded it's no earthly good.

It is no accident that the term "reflection" is generally used in organizing to refer to the theological task. It is not called a discussion. Nor is it a debate. Theology as carried out in faith-based organizing is always theoretical reflection upon practice.

As stated earlier, when clergy who are engaged in community organizing are brought together, it is most often called a "caucus." This term also is intentional. Drawn from the political world rather than from academia, to speak of a clergy caucus is to point to a way of doing theology. A caucus is a setting for religious leaders to reflect theologically upon their experience of relating faith to the public square.

The homework for one regional clergy caucus I attended illustrates how theology is approached in community organizing. Each of the participants was asked to reflect in advance on three basic questions. How has organizing influenced my congregation? How has organizing influenced my ministry? How has organizing influenced my self?

The following four chapters are devoted to the fundamental concepts that serve as the foundation for faith-based community organizing: Self-Interest, Power, Relationships, and Values. Implicit to the approach I take is responding to the above questions, blended together, of how organizing has personally influenced my ministry context.

I have tried for some time to visualize the inter-relationship of these four. I have seen this illustrated by a triangle, with values in the center. Sometimes it shows up as a square with each concept being one of the four corners. And on occasion it appears as a circle with one flowing into the other in a cyclical pattern.

What I have come up with instead is an image that hopefully suggests, in abridged form, the symbol for nuclear energy. To me it says that all four concepts are dynamically inter-related. Like an atomic force field, there is a synergistic energy that results from holding these four together in tension. A particular polarity between self-interest and values is visualized, as between power and relationships. But as part of one unitary fusion called faith-based organizing, each of the four is dynamically related to each one of the other concepts.

Chapters 10-13 address these foundational concepts by reflecting theologically upon each one with respect to my experience in the congregation, in ministry, and in my own personal/spiritual growth. I plan to show how self-interest, power, relationships, and values are all bound together in creating the highly energized, even creatively explosive, activity I have known in ministry as an organizing pastor. Chapter 14—Jesus' Organizing Strategy—is offered as an example of a reflection given at a clergy caucus. Chapter 15—Telling the Story in a New Way—explores what it looks like to take on the role of organizing pastor.

This second part of the book is an invitation to others to continue reflecting upon the values that drive faith-based community organizing by speaking from lived experience. In my understanding it is theology in praxis that is most useful to the religious practitioner. I imagine that this would also apply to community organizers and others who work closely with leaders of congregations. The following reflections are offered as a guide to the reader to participate in the same activity. By engaging in this disciplined process I think there is a realistic expectation that, like the prophet Habakkuk, we might together "write the vision and make it plain" in the communities we serve.

Chapter 10

SELF-INTEREST 'PROPERLY UNDERSTOOD'

"You have a good heart and you think the good thing is to be guilty and kind but it's not always kind to be gentle and soft, there's a genuine violence softness and kindness visit on people. Sometimes self-interested is the most generous thing you can be. "
— Tony Kushner (Angels in America, Part Two: Perestroika)

"The doctrine of self-interest properly understood is not new, but it has been universally accepted by today's Americans. ... (This) is not a very lofty doctrine, but it is a clear and reliable one. ... By itself it is incapable of making a man virtuous, but it does create a multitude of citizens who are disciplined, temperate, moderate, prudent, and self-controlled."
[Alexis de Tocqueville]

The four foundational concepts of faith-based community organizing are all inter-related. One could start anywhere and end up at the beginning point. So why begin with self-interest?

I had been asked to lead reflections at a regional clergy

caucus on these concepts. And so I invited suggestions from the group as to where we should begin. One person immediately nominated relationships, saying that what distinguished faith-based organizing from a secular approach was an emphasis upon the relational. Others suggested values for a similar reason. It so happened that no one advocated starting with power. What I vividly recall is that the two organizers present, one of whom is also ordained clergy, quietly proposed self-interest.

While we could begin with any of the four foundational concepts, I think it is especially appropriate to start off with self-interest. This tends to be the most difficult for people of faith, with power possibly coming in a close second. Tackling the tough one up front might make the rest of this exercise a bit easier. Besides, there is no possibility of effectively participating in the political sphere without taking self-interest seriously. Ever since Saul Alinsky launched his project in Chicago in the late 1930s, the starting-point in community organizing has been an appeal to self-interest.

This is highly problematic in faith-based organizing for some obvious reasons. Each of our religious traditions affirms the importance of being for others. A definition of sin is when one's own ego is placed at the center of the universe. An emphasis upon self-interest, therefore, appears at first glance to be antithetical to the religious enterprise. This makes it all the more essential that the concept lying at the heart of community organizing, and of all political activity, be critiqued theologically. Unless we can make sense of self-interest as a positive dimension of living faithfully, organizing will not—should not—be entertained as an enterprise appropriate for our congregations, our ministries, our souls.

There is something raw and real about the concept of self-interest. Beginning elsewhere can take the edge off what is unique about community organizing. And that includes organizing that is centered in the life of religious congregations, organizing that is *faith-based.*

By the same token, I don't think it helps, at least as we begin the discussion, to qualify it as *enlightened* self-interest. Tocqueville's qualifier is preferable: "Self-interest *properly understood.*" But the way I first learned the term in theological seminary in the early 1960s, and how until recently I've generally used it as a preacher over the years—enlightened self-interest—is less than adequate. Christian ethics speaks of self-interest in nuanced ways for good reasons. Self-interest, devoid of relationships and values, is crass and self-serving. But to begin with "enlightened" smoothes over the rough and tough reality of human experience. It might make the term more palatable, but does so at the expense of turning it into a vague spiritualization.

As mentioned in Chapter 1, I vividly recall my first serious encounter with faith-based community organizing. What was to become Inland Congregations United for Change had just hired its first Director-Organizer who was now calling on me as a participating pastor. After the opening pleasantries, Pat Kennedy cut to the quick. "What is your church's self-interest?" Somewhat taken aback by this jolting question which appeared to challenge the purity of my congregation's and my own altruistic motives, I responded by saying in so many words that we were interested in helping those less fortunate than ourselves. That selflessness is a Christian virtue. That it is more blessed to give than to receive… You know the litany.

"Yes, but," Pat continued, "what is YOUR interest as a pastor in all of this?" I can't say I liked the direction this was going. I was even less prepared to answer this question. After all, isn't ministry supposed to be a selfless act of giving ourselves to others—to God, to the church, to the community?

It was this self-interest question, however troubling as it was, that hooked me on organizing. It planted a seed that would help to transform my life and ministry into what I believe to be a more faithful and effective witness.

+ + + + +

So what is self-interest as we define it in congregation, faith-based, community organizing? I think it helps to begin with what it is not.

It is *not* the opposite of altruistic selflessness. Religious folk are commonly accused, too often with accuracy, of being sentimental and ineffective in the face of the huge challenges facing the world today. Many years ago the title of an article by Ivan Illich caught my attention: "The Seamy Side of Charity." It was a critique of the plan to send thousands of Catholic missionaries from the United States to Latin America. Illich argued that the church must face "the painful side of generosity: the burden that a life gratuitously offered imposes on the recipient." Even if unconscious, a do-gooder mentality can create unhealthy dependencies. A minister-friend of mine puts it even more bluntly: "If someone says he wants to help you, run like hell!"

One organizing principle states this as an iron rule: *Never do for others what they can do for themselves.* As important and as essential as charity is in relieving symptoms, it fails to address root causes. An appreciation of self-interest moves the focus from the short-term delivery of emergency services to the long-term building of community. It is like the old adage about giving a man a fish and he will be fed once. Teach him to fish and he will feed himself (and his community) for the rest of his life.

Self-interest is *not* the same as selfishness or self-centeredness. Because our culture practically worships the cult of radical individualism, neglecting the public sphere in which life is shared with others, self-interest is frequently vilified as a source of the problem. This is, however, a misunderstanding of the concept. Selfishness, or self-centeredness, is a more accurate term for that which plagues modern life today. Reinhold Niebuhr describes evil as self-interest lived outside of its proper context. "Evil is always the assertion of some self-interest without regard to the whole, whether the whole be conceived as the immediate community, or the total community of mankind, or the total order of the world."[1]

Self-interest as understood in community organizing, on the other hand, is the healthy acknowledgment of one's own individual limits and capacities. It is simply and profoundly an awareness that all significant change, personal and social, is rooted in a centered self. Indeed the very possibility of building human community is dependent upon free relationships among separate, distinct, unique selves, each of which is a center of interests reflecting needs, values, and purposes. Self-interest, in other words, is the point of access to discerning community-interest. Grounded in democratic and religious values, this first organizing concept provides a pathway to what people of faith pray for—the building of a *community* of self-interests.

So, if neither selflessness nor selfishness, why is self-interest an important starting point for understanding *faith-based* community organizing?

Self-interest is grounded theologically in the affirmation that each person is made in the image of God. In the first biblical Creation story, God says, "Let us make *adam*—humankind—in our image..." [Genesis 1:26] For Christians, it is our relationship with the Christ—the new *adam* [Romans 5:12-21; First Corinthians 15:20-49]—whose life of self-giving love calls each of us to new life as unique, irreplaceable, powerful persons. Without a self that has interests, there can be no self-giving.

Even prior to that, self-interest is grounded in an understanding of who God is. The biblical faith tradition speaks of ultimate reality in personal terms. God is a "self" with interests. The sacred name of YHWH (written in many English Bibles as "LORD," spelled in all-capital letters) revealed to Moses on

Mount Sinai—the unique term appearing thousands of times in the Bible, far more than any other name for God in the Hebrew Scriptures—can be translated literally as "I AM WHO I AM." Or, "I WILL BE WHAT I WILL BE." [Exodus 3:14] To be a child of God is to be the creation of a personal divinity who is an "I"—who is a Self.

The second Creation story also speaks of the human being as a self with interests. God takes the *adam* (literally "from the earth") and breathes into this human form the breath of life, creating a *nephesh,* a living soul. [Genesis 2:7] This physical-emotional-spiritual totality that is the human being often is translated as "self" or "person." This living soul—this self—hungers and thirsts, not only physically, but emotionally and spiritually. This living soul feels joy, sorrow, love, hope, anger, despair.

To be human, in other words, is to be created as a self with interests. Far deeper than what is commonly referred to as physical and psychological needs, these interests flow out of the passionate center that makes us human. Staying with the poetry of the Creation narrative, self-interest is the breath of God manifested in the individual person. It is the divine breath of life—like artificial respiration—that is breathed into the inanimate human form, making it a self. Our self-interests are as close to us as the very air we breathe.

But there is more to the biblical understanding of what constitutes a living soul—what makes up a self. In the anthropology of the Bible, a person is not only a psychosomatic unity, but also exists in a social and historical context. Systems theory speaks both of how the whole is made up of the sum of its parts, and of how each individual part contains the whole within it. So also, the self contains within it the larger social/historical world in which it exists. Rather than isolated, the self is related. As the organizing principle states, *self-interest is always relational.*

Ancient Israel affirmed this in remembering its origins in slavery. The Decalogue, the Ten Commandments, is introduced with a reminder of where the people of the Bible had come from. "Then God spoke all these words: 'I am the LORD your God, who brought you out of the land of Egypt, out of the house of slavery; (therefore) you shall have no other gods before me..." [Exodus 20:1-3] To this day, thousands of years after the exodus from Egypt, when a Jewish family sits at table to observe *Pesach* (Passover), the traditional words from Deuteronomy are spoken to remind everyone present of their identity. "When your children ask you in time to come, 'What is the meaning of the decrees and the statutes and the ordinances that the LORD our God has commanded you?' then you shall say to your children, 'We were Pharaoh's slaves in Egypt, but the LORD brought us out of Egypt with a mighty hand...'" [Deuteronomy 6:20-21]

In the same way, racial and ethnic identity is not external to a person, but is an essential dimension of one's self. Socio-economic class is likewise integral to an understanding of who a person is. Family and social history constitute part of one's self. The self is a historical being, and our self-interests are always an expression of our family histories.

This was powerfully expressed at a regional clergy caucus when one Baptist pastor spoke of how self-interest for him begins with his primary reality of being African-American, male, and Christian, living in 21st century imperial America. For him, in his words, life is lived at the "intersection" between individual self-interest and communal self-interest.

It was again articulated when a Catholic priest testified how his self-interest arose out of his historically conditioned self. Half of his family had been farm workers in Hawaii and incarcerated during World War II. Immigration reform was, therefore, of intense interest for him. Its roots in his soul, in his words, were almost "genetic" in nature. Self-interest was a matter of "ancestral recall."

Another pastor spoke of his relatively privileged family having been "valley farmers" in the San Joaquin Valley for over a hundred years. Self-interest was a matter of truth-telling, of being transparent, and happily discovering in the process that deep spiritual wells unknown to him in earlier years were now abundantly and powerfully present.

Self-interest is to organizing what motivation is to psychology. Another community organizing principle: *Self-interest moves people.* It opens the window into our hurt and feelings of injustice, our desires and passions. The human organism not only seeks to relieve pain but requires that injustice as it is experienced be redressed. Once a person's interests have been brought to the surface they do not need to be persuaded by another to act. One is then moved internally by forces from within. Just as a self grows and changes over time, its interests are not static. They dynamically adapt to changing circumstances. Therefore, to complete this principle: *Self-interest changes.*

Self-interest is the very opposite of altruistic selflessness on one extreme or selfish self-centeredness on the other. It is, rather, the stuff out of which human community is built. Rabbi Hillel the Elder who lived in the first century BCE stated as clearly as anyone the dynamic inter-relationship between self-interest and an urgent commitment to build human community. "If I am not for myself, who will be for me? If I am only for myself, what am I? If not now, when?"

A word study of "interest" further points to this social and relational dimension of the first organizing concept. Its Latin origins—*interesse*—reveal a combination of two words: "to be" *(esse)* and "between" *(inter).* To have interest is to be between, to take part in. The Indo-European root of *es* leads us even further into the world of inter-connectedness. Important derivations include "am, is, yes, essence." (Curiously, by negative example, even "sin"—the very breakdown of interconnectedness—is a derivative.) Self-interest, according to its etymology, implies being and existing, describing what is real and true. It depicts the passionate center of a human being as one strives to be meaningfully connected with one's own inner life, with the larger community, and with the ancestral community.

Douglas Hofstadter tells of how the self is relational from his perspective as a cognitive scientist. He begins with a personal story of how he discovered the degree to which he had been influenced by his wife, Carol, who had died of a brain tumor when she was only forty-two. Months later, when he was looking at a picture of Carol, he felt he was behind her eyes and all at once was saying, through tears, "That's me. That's me." More than mere influence, however, he acknowledges how his wife physically had become part of him—"about the fusion of our souls into one higher level entity, about the fact that at the core of both our souls lay identical hopes and dreams for our children, about the notion that those hopes were not separate or distinct hopes but were just one hope, one clear thing that defined us both, that wielded us into a unit, the kind of unit I had but dimly imagined before being married and having children." Hofstadter's understanding of the self is that it is a point of view, a way of seeing the world. It emerges from the conglomeration of all the flares, loops and perceptions that have been shared and developed with others.[2]

In faith-based community organizing self-interest is understood in a similar way. It is a point of view, a way of seeing the world. The beginning place for organizing is to take seriously how a person sees the world. Because the self is not an isolated atom, but is always part of a relational "loop," one doesn't stop here. How a person sees the world is an entry point to identifying the interests of his or her family, of the surrounding neighborhood, of the larger community. By beginning with self-interest, the process leads to the discernment of a community of self-interest.

\+ + + + +

When the organizer was confronting me with questions of my self-interest, I was aware of these distinctions on an intellectual level. But it was my involvement in our organizing project that moved my awareness from head to heart.

In 1990, when I began a new pastorate in San Bernardino, the congregation had little understanding of its self-interests. It wanted to grow, of course. What organization, what organism, doesn't want to grow and thrive? But discerning the self-interests of the congregation is not the same as doing needs assessments and developing market-based programs. It means paying attention to the "living souls" who constitute the community of faith. It means careful and disciplined listening to the spirit-breath animating the people of God.

Membership had been gradually declining for years. Financial support was diminishing. It had grown isolated from its immediate neighborhood. I was shocked to learn when talking with people down the street and small business owners in the neighborhood who passed by our building each day on their way to work that they didn't even realize we were a church. The fellowship life of the church was exceptionally strong, and the membership continued to be selflessly generous in its support of denominational and local charities. But little attention was given to building up its own life. By persistent questioning of church leaders about what we considered to be our congregation's self-interests, we began to pay much greater attention to the personal stories of our own present members. What were their hungers and thirsts, their joys and their sorrows? Through an intentional one-to-one listening process we identified what congregants were passionate about, what it was that made life for them worth living.

Our immediate neighborhood was no longer perceived as alien, but as the context for our life and future. One-to-one visits were made with neighbors, not to promote our church program, but to listen to their personal stories. What were they concerned about living in San Bernardino? What had changed for them since they first moved here, and how has this impacted upon their family? What did they feel so strongly about that they would be willing to meet with others in the neighborhood to do something about it? In other words, but without necessarily using these words at the time, what is their self-interest?

The church continued to be generous in its mission support of denominational work and local service agencies. However, a strategic change took place as self-interest of the congregation was being paid attention to. A significant portion of the outreach dollars were shifted from charity to community organizing in recognition that our congregation was being strengthened in the process—through the tangible support in leadership development that we received from our organizer, as well as the deepened ties with ecumenical partners and our increased visibility in the larger community. Organizing not only helped us to identify our congregation's self-interest, but organizing itself came to be clearly recognized and appreciated as being in our self-interest.

I also came to realize, in looking back over the years of serving churches in many places, that I had carelessly been confusing my own self-interest as a pastor with the interests of the congregation. This is, of course, neither healthy nor helpful. On the one hand it can too easily lead to an unconscious imposition of one's will upon the congregation. On the other hand, and more importantly in my own situation, it can lead to an entire ministry being absorbed by the congregation's needs at the expense of the pastor's own interests. Sometimes it was difficult for me to tell which was which. I came to realize that I had my own pastoral self-interests that were distinct from those of the congregation. Fortunately, they were for the most part compatible. Otherwise, there would be no possibility of doing ministry together. But there were times prior to my ministry in San Bernardino, I realize in retrospect, that I had accepted a call that was not good for my health. Our interests were not really compatible.

Happily, this final pastorate in San Bernardino before retirement was the most satisfying of all. An appreciation of self-interests helped me to be clearer about boundaries. Although I have always enjoyed being a pastor, none was more rewarding than the last. I attribute this in no small part to being clear about my own self-interests as a pastor.

And there is more to my life, of course, than my vocation as a pastor. I am also married (it took me twice to get it right), I am a father (of children now long gone from the nest), I have friends outside my congregation who have been my lifeline on many an occasion (mostly clergy who, not incidentally, for the most part are organizing pastors from other denominations). I like to keep physically active and am increasingly dealing with an awareness of my mortality as time marches on. And, most importantly, I have a soul. Or more accurately, I am a soul, a living soul. It is in my self-interest to nurture each of these relationships—with family and friends, with my aging mind and body, with God. Indeed, my life depends upon my paying attention to this personal/spiritual self-interest. In retirement, as in the days of active ministry, my most fundamental self-interest is to make certain that my well does not dry up. If it ever does, I'll have nothing to give to anyone else. And I'll have no one to blame but myself.

Chapter 11

POWERLESSNESS CORRUPTS

"God did not give us a spirit of cowardice,
but rather a spirit of power and of love and of self-discipline."
[Second Timothy 1:6-7]

"Our deepest fear is not that we are inadequate.
Our deepest fear is that we are powerful beyond measure."
[Nelson Mandela, from his inaugural speech, 1994]

The second foundational concept dynamically shaping congregation, faith-based, community organizing is *POWER.* This naturally flows from a consideration of self-interest. To be a spirit-filled human being—a living soul, an actualized self—is to be a center of power.

In the faith community and in our culture at large, power is perhaps as problematic as self-interest. In contrast to popular culture and some of traditional Christian theology, power is understood in community organizing to be essentially good. Quite simply and profoundly, as an organizing principle defines the concept, *power is the ability to act.* To be sure, power can be misused and abused. Equally serious is that it can be squandered through non-use or under-use. But power itself is a gift from God, and therefore good.

An appreciation of power, and the diagnostic ability to analyze how power is being used in a particular setting, is key to any engagement in the political sphere. For that matter, it is required for functioning effectively in the ecclesiastical sphere. Living healthily in a family is no exception to this rule.

I recall an experience I had over 45 years ago in theological seminary. The drama department was producing Luigi Pirandello's play, "Lazarus." Set in 20th century Italy, the story is centered on a person who had a heart attack and was declared dead. Moments later—as in the gospel story of the raising of Lazarus, although a considerably briefer time duration than the four days reported in the Bible—he came back to life having to face others who had already considered him dead.

I had been cast in the role of the Monsignor. The problem was, I didn't know how to act like one. The director kept working with me to act with authority—through my voice, my gestures, in the subtlety of movement. I think I finally got it. But it was tough going. I simply didn't feel comfortable at that time of life taking on the role of someone who was in a position of power.

Not that I did not actually have power. What business do I have talking to anyone else about this subject given my social position? After all, I am a person of privilege—educated, male, white, middle class, American. No thanks to my own doing, I had been profoundly entitled as a person of power in our society—one who, relatively effortlessly, was able to accomplish most of what I set out to do. In those early days I was somewhat embarrassed about this power. On one level it was a matter of innocence that, of course, does not let anyone off the hook. After all these years I know that my innocence was an expression of something else. By not acknowledging the power I had, I did not have to assume full responsibility for how I used it. Which is to say, I was not using it wisely some of the time. And I certainly was not using it to the fullest of my capacity to become all that God had created me to be.

There is considerable ambivalence in our society about power. This was reflected in a conversation I once had with my daughter. She was claiming that power was neutral, neither good nor bad. She had a point, of course, since power in practice can be used in either good or bad ways. But I felt she wasn't taking it seriously enough, that she was trying to wiggle out of having to assume responsibility for the considerable power she had. So I kept trying to make the point that power itself is *essentially* good.

This same ambivalence—whether power is good, bad, or indifferent—is manifested in liturgical prayers and religious literature. The Lord's Prayer concludes (when the doxological ending is included, as is the universal practice in Protestant churches) with an unqualified affirmation of the power of God: "For thine is the kingdom and the power and the glory for ever." In another prayer, this one for world peace, there is again a positive value associated with power: "Look, we beseech thee, upon thy family of nations and men, to whom thou hast committed power in trust for their mutual health and well-being."

But then, by contrast, another traditional prayer speaks of power as something to be forsaken: "Lord Jesus Christ, you left behind you all power and security." A devotional resource I was following at one time included a meditation titled "Power and Love." Unfortunately, in my opinion, power was defined as the polar opposite of love. There are two ways of life, the meditation counseled. Power and love, and only one of them is Christ's way. The concrete illustrations offered for each of these two ways of life were actually quite helpful. In the first way there is a need to control and be invulnerable, obviously serious obstacles to a healthy life. The second way calls for openness to friendship and intimacy. But the point here is that it is a mistake to use the word "power" exclusively to refer to the wrong spiritual path. It contributes to ambivalence about power among religious folk. It would be more helpful to speak of the "love of power" versus the "power of love." When power and love are pitted against one another, however, and Christ's way is identified solely with the latter, the two are not on a level playing field. It takes little imagination to guess which one of the two is recommended in this meditation, and what happens to power according to this definition.[1]

The argument finally comes down to a matter of faith. How does one understand power theologically?

\+ + + + +

To believe in God is to affirm the goodness of all creation. Everything that exists came into being, and is daily re-created, by God's power. "Then God said, 'Let there be light', and there was light. And God saw that the light was good." In theology, as in physics, light is power. God is the one ultimately "able to act" to accomplish the divine will. To be human, made in the "image" of God, is to share God's gift of power. To have been given "dominion" (a political metaphor) is to have been gifted with the ability to act so as to be able to care for creation as God intends. [Genesis 1:1ff.]

The "living self" *(nephesh)* created by the breath of God animating the first *adam* is a center of power. It is a center of the ability to act. To be actualized as a human being is to be powerful. As the theologian Paul Tillich observes, "Every self is a power structure."[2]

This power can, of course, be destructive. That is surely why there is commonly such ambivalence about the term. Our experience of power, especially in its most dramatic manifestations, frequently is that it is anything but good. The Bible is no stranger to this awareness. From the earliest pages of scripture there is testimony to the human abuse of God's good gift of power. A definition of sin—that which separates human beings from God, from one another, and from one's own self—is, quite simply, the abuse of power. But power itself, as part of God's created order, is good. Ancient legends describe demons as fallen angels. They were originally agents of God. But when they chose to use their power in ways other than to serve God's purposes, they became demonic forces.

Glenn Tinder points to selfishness as a human choice that distorts the goodness of power. "Power is not necessarily used for selfish purposes. If it ordinarily is, that is due to the selfishness of those who use it, not to the character of power."[3]

The Apostle Paul speaks of "principalities and powers" as a historical manifestation of evil. It is power turned bad—a demonic force incarnated in human institutions. It is that which God's love will ultimately prevail over. "For I am convinced that neither death, nor life, nor angels, nor principalities (rulers), nor things present, nor things to come, nor powers, nor height, nor depth, nor anything else in all creation, will be able to separate us from the love of God in Christ Jesus our Lord." [Romans 8: 38-39]

Walter Wink writes of how "the Powers" are both spiritual and institutional. The multivalent understanding of power as something essentially good, yet horrifically evil, is addressed by Wink in his three volume series on Engaging, Naming, and Unmasking the Powers. His summary of the thesis underlying the entire series speaks to the challenge of dealing with this second foundational concept of faith-based community organizing: "The Powers are good. The Powers are fallen. The Powers must be redeemed."[4]

Fallen power is dehumanizing. When internalized it destroys

the soul. When a person has been the subject of abuse, the power to control and dehumanize can take root like an invisible cancer eating away at one's sense of worth. As the saying goes: "It's one thing to take Israel out of Egypt, but it's a lot more difficult to take Egypt (slavery, domination, powerlessness) out of Israel."

Paulo Freire, in his *Pedagogy of the Oppressed,* tells how a person who is part of an oppressed social class—a group having little or virtually no official power—internalizes the source of oppression. "The oppressed, having internalized the image of the oppressor and adopted his guidelines, are fearful of freedom. ... They are at one and the same time themselves and the oppressor whose consciousness they have internalized." [5] They even tend to blame themselves for their misfortunes, assuming that they themselves are responsible for their own poverty and exploitation. This is the inner-oppressor at work. It is easier to take a person out of an abusive situation than it is to take the abuser out of the abused. In such instances when power is abused, it is a manifestation of evil. Such power dehumanizes individuals and perpetuates systems of exploitation. The challenge for persons who feel powerless is first to become aware of their own situation, and secondly to join with others in building a powerful organization able to stand over and against the power that is oppressing them.

The oppressor also is dehumanized in this process, Friere states. While he does not literally use the term, it is as if he is also developing a "pedagogy of the oppressor." What is required is a new relationship with one's own power and privilege on the one hand, and on the other hand with the persons in society who do not have this same access to power. Paternalistic treatment of others will not help, nor will guilt. Both attitudes perpetuate the cycles of abuse. Rather, a "radical posture" is called for in which one who is privileged stands with and alongside those who are oppressed. "Solidarity requires that one enter into the situation of those with whom one is solidary. ... The oppressor is solidary with the oppressed only when he stops regarding the oppressed as an abstract category and sees them as persons who have been unjustly dealt with, deprived of their voice, cheated in the sale of their labor—when he stops making pious, sentimental, and individualistic gestures and risks an act of love."[6]

Community organizing provides a context in which such acts of love can be risked. Although faith-based organizing most often takes root in congregations made up of persons who are marginalized from the centers of established power, congregations of the relatively privileged also can and do become engaged. Paternalism is avoided by taking self-interest seriously. Likewise, guilt does not function as an operating principle because of the focus upon using one's own power wisely. In my own pastoral experience, faith-based community organizing provides a setting like none other where rich and poor, Black and White, Hispanic and Anglo can effectively stand with and work alongside one another in building a powerful human community that is in the interest of everyone.

That is because power is relational. As another organizing principle states this concept, *power is in the relationship.* To speak of power as relational is to affirm that it is grounded in justice-love, not force. Another word for relational is spiritual. Spiritual power, although distinct from coercive force, is nevertheless real power. It is the ability to act in every dimension of life—spiritually, emotionally, politically.

Paul Tillich analyzes the relationship among *Love, Power, and Justice* in a little book with this title. He speaks of the unity of these three in personal relations, group relations, and ultimate relations. It is when power is separated from love and justice that it becomes demonic. While there are tensions among the three, Tillich states, they are ontologically bound together, each existing only in relation to the others. "Love, power, and justice are united in God, and they are united in the new creation of God in the world."[7]

Power, as it is used in faith-based community organizing, is not for the sake of accumulating power, but is purposeful. It is grounded in democratic and religious values. In the Christian tradition power is ultimately expressed through the life and ministry of Jesus. In the words of one pastor participating in a clergy caucus, "Christ, the most powerful person in the world, is the model for power." This is clearly an alternative vision of power than dominant culture affirms. On the face of it, Jesus is not successful, but is defeated. And yet this is real power. It is an ability to act that is socially transformative. The Apostle Paul argued that "the cross of Christ not be emptied of its power." [First Corinthians 1:17] In speaking of the power of the cross—an instrument of torture and execution—Paul was pointing to the powerful organization that was created as a consequence of Christ's life and ministry, death and resurrection—the church as a community of faith. Jesus and Paul were community organizers. They bequeathed to the world powerful organizations able to transform the structure of human existence. The power of the cross that is manifested in the church is one and the same as resurrection power—the ability to transform life, individually and in social-economic structures, according to God's purposes of governance based upon justice-love.

Again, to quote the pastor who spoke of Christ as the model for power, "Real power is standing in the midst of community, to *be* in the midst of the ambiguity of life."

\+ + + + +

Community organizing identifies essentially two kinds of power in the political arena. As the organizing principle states: *power is organized money, and power is organized people.* It is obvious which of these two is most accessible to religious congregations and the families of the larger community that they serve. If a hint is needed, consider this. It is not money.

There is real power that is organized when congregations come together to push an action with a public official. There is something heady about the experience—hundreds, if not thousands, of ordinary families in one place, speaking face-to-face on an equal footing with the mayor or the governor—making demands, pinning commitments, following through. That is why there is an "assessment" at the conclusion of every organizing meeting—whether it be the local organizing committee or a federated action. There are the usual evaluative questions about how well it worked, who did what and how well, what was accomplished, what are the next steps. But the fundamental question is: did we use our power responsibly? We not only hold others accountable for the power entrusted to them in the public sphere, but we are required to critique our own use of power. The well-known aphorism about the ability of power to corrupt applies to ourselves as well.

Power analysis is an essential component of all political activity. This is reflected in a number of principles, or aphorisms, used by community organizers. One way to illustrate this is to relate them to the relatively mild clash of power manifested in the opening story in Chapter 1 about the action in San Bernardino. *Real power is often hidden.* The way of doing business in the city for as long as anyone could remember was for well-connected individuals behind the scenes to lean on an elected official with whom they had a personal relationship. It could be difficult knowing who those people were who had easy access to the mayor and council. *Power defines the rules.* The implicit "rule" was that ordinary families without connection, other than having the occasional opportunity to vote, had no role in setting public policy that of necessity is always done between elections. The powerful action redefined this rule.

Power respects power was demonstrated in the success of the community organization to get the mayor and several additional public officials to attend a mass meeting. This had never happened before. There was considerable resistance and there were attempts to derail the meeting in advance. But the prospect of a thousand citizens assembled and organized to state its agenda got results. Coming from religious congregations with the strong support of clergy leadership added the power of a moral voice to these demands to support the community's youth. *Power is taken, not given.* Permission to bring these concerns was not asked for. As was their right as citizens of the community, they did not simply request the attention of their elected leaders, but demanded it. Respect was given to the mayor, but he was not deferred to as a superior. By assembling in a religious sanctuary where the community organization was in control of the meeting, rather than in city hall where the mayor leads the meetings, clearly established who was in charge.

Finally, as the organizing principle affirms about power: *Use it or lose it.* Setting a follow up meeting with the mayor for a progress report was only the first of a series of steps taken to use the power that had been built leading up to the action. The organization could not rest on its laurels or it would lose what it had gained. So it continued the same process as before of doing one-to-ones, identifying new issues, and using their growing power to give voice to the ordinary families of the community in the public square.

The power of a congregation is considerable. God has gifted it with all the power required to carry out its mission. Especially when linked with the power of other congregations in a federated action, there is nothing external that can prevent our "ability to act" effectively on behalf of ordinary families.

So why do congregations and clergy so often complain of feeling powerless? This suggests another organizing principle: *powerlessness corrupts.* Michael Lerner's concept of "surplus powerlessness" points us in the direction of understanding this bewilderment. There are, in reality, seemingly overwhelming obstacles standing in the way of addressing the concerns of ordinary families. With the extreme concentration of wealth that is increasing in our economy, a few have vast power to shape economic and political decisions while most are relatively powerless. Lerner calls this "*real* powerlessness." But, as Lerner argues, this does not account for why people are usually so reluctant to develop the power they actually have. He calls this phenomenon "*surplus* powerlessness." It is a matter of belief—wrong belief. It is the set of feelings and beliefs that make people think of themselves as even more powerless than the actual power situation requires, and then leads them to act in ways that actually confirm them in their powerlessness. In a clever paraphrasing of Lord Acton's famous saying—"Power tends to corrupt, and absolute power corrupts absolutely"—Lerner states that power*lessness* corrupts. "Powerlessness corrupts in a very direct way: It changes, transforms, and distorts us. It makes us different from how we would otherwise want to be. We look at our world and our own behavior, and we tell ourselves that although we really aren't living the lives we want to live, there is nothing we can do about it. We are powerless."[8]

Why is there so frequently such a surplus of powerlessness within religious congregations? Perhaps it is caused by a lack of conviction. Oftentimes it is brought about by lack of organization or imagination. But most importantly, I think it reflects a refusal to assume responsibility for the considerable power the congregation has been given. The feeling of powerlessness is a crisis of faith. Denying the power that we actually have, whether through innocence or lack of courage, is a denial of the powerful God who has created us and who calls us to be powerful agents of justice-love in this world.[9]

And why is it that clergy so often feel powerless? Why is there such a surplus of powerlessness among those who have been entrusted with the symbols of ultimate power? To be sure, as all of our faith traditions have recently had to come to terms with in dealing with clergy malpractice, the abuse of power is a shameful blot upon our respective witnesses to God's justice-love. This is a sinful distortion of God's good gift of life, of sexuality, of power. We have come to understand that abuse in any form, including domestic violence, is not so much about sex as it is about power. It is essential that we hold ourselves accountable for the power we exercise as clergy. Otherwise we can hardly hold public officials accountable for the power entrusted to them.

But is not the feeling of powerlessness also a sin? Could it be that even the abuse of power on the part of clergy is a twisted form of a profound sense of impotency? By office and training and personal charisma, however, each clergyperson in reality has been gifted with power. We know the familiar words from Second Timothy associated by so many of us with our ordination vows: "I remind you to rekindle the gift of God that is within you through the laying on of my hands; for God did not give us a spirit of cowardice, but rather a spirit of power and of love and of self-discipline." [Second Timothy 1:6-7] As grossly unacceptable as the abuse of clergy power is, I wonder if the greater sin is not the failure responsibly to use fully the power that has been entrusted to us. Sins of omission are as serious as sins of commission. If only we were holding ourselves as accountable for power squandered as for power abused.

We have been gifted, as children of God, with the power to be, to live joyfully and purposefully, to love justly and responsibly. It is our living souls that are at stake as we live with the power entrusted to us. Surplus powerlessness can kill the soul as well as the body. And so we pray. Prayer is a powerful act. Because power is in the relationship—with God.

Chapter 12

RELATIONSHIPS THAT GO SOMEWHERE

> *"I love the LORD, because he has heard my voice and my supplications. Because God inclined his ear to me, therefore will I call on him as long as I live."*
> [Psalm 116:1-2]

> *"All real living is meeting."*
> [Martin Buber]

Accountability for the power we have moves us directly into considering the third foundational concept for faith-based community organizing—*RELATIONSHIPS*. Accountability means responsibility. Responsibility—the ability to respond—implies relationships. We have already hinted at the importance of relationships in the organizing principle that *power is in the relationship*. It is time now to take a closer look at relationship itself.

This emphasis upon the centrality of relationships is what makes organizing such a good fit for clergy. One of the central organizing principles is the importance of asking: *Whom do you love?* Every religious leader worth his or her salt knows that the most important thing to do in beginning a new ministry, before introducing any major changes, is to get to know the congregation. I learned this the hard way long after I should have known better. I had even been reminded of this at a service of installation as a minister friend, a generation older than I, delivered the charge to the pastor: "Let them know you love them." I did love them, but I didn't let them know it.

Prior to my pastoral experience of community organizing—after I had been serving churches for almost a quarter century—I accepted a call that was the biggest challenge I had faced up to that point. The search committee had identified numerous issues facing the church that the new minister would hopefully be able to help them address. All had a sense of urgency about them. I promptly got to the task and in fact succeeded in addressing everything on the list, cramming about ten years of projects into two. This was not, however, a rewarding ministry. The basic reason was because I had not taken the time to get to know the congregation. I failed to develop strong and trusting relationships with the membership. I didn't let them know I loved them.

\+ + + + +

The beginning point for a theology of relationship is God's covenant. A covenant is a relationship based on personal choice, commitment and trust. In the biblical faith tradition it is God who initiates this primary relationship. The story of Noah speaks of a covenant with the created order and all of humankind. [Genesis 9:8-17] With all future covenants a human response freely given is required to complete it. God enters into covenant with Abraham to be the ancestor of a multitude of nations through whom all the peoples of the world will be blessed. [Genesis 17:1-22] God remembers the covenant when the Hebrew slaves cry out [Exodus 2:23-25] and establishes a covenant on Mt. Sinai with the Israelites. [Exodus 24:1-8] Central to the Eucharistic liturgy of the church is the covenant initiated by God in Jesus Christ. [Mark 14:22-25]

The term "covenant" appears over 400 times in the Bible. It affirms that all of existence is relational and that life is lived in relationship. This relationship is ethical with each party having obligations to the other. Key to the prophetic message is calling the people of God to accountability for their covenantal obligations. The biblical story tells of the covenant being broken by the people, and God who is merciful and compassionate renewing it again and again. It is in this relationship with God that humans receive an identity, become a people, and discover meaning. This relationship is purposeful; it goes somewhere.

To be part of God's covenant binds the people to one another. There is no relationship with God possible apart from a relationship with others in the covenant community. There are no isolated individuals, only persons living in covenant with one another. This covenant creates a "we" in which persons have moral obligations toward one another in the community they share. And because of God's creation and love of all the peoples of the earth, being part of God's covenant binds one to all the human family. Correspondingly, we have moral obligations to live justly with all persons. The corporate reality of being a "we" extends to all the human community.

Creation exists only in relationship with the Creator. The first Creation story in the Bible states that human beings are created in "the image of God." [Genesis 1:22] This is not in the absurd sense of being made to look like God, like some kind of sculptured representation. That would make humans into idols. Rather, the *imago dei* is a relational term. In the ancient world when the king would send his soldiers out to the farther reaches of the kingdom, they would be led by someone holding up an emblem— *imago*— of the royal office. This would signify to the local inhabitants that this military unit was acting under the king's authority and that it represented his presence. For humans to be created in the image of God, therefore, affirms that our humanity lies in our relationship with the Creator. Take away the relationship, with God and with one another, and we cease to be human.

Today this relational dimension of existence is being affirmed through virtually every intellectual discipline. For example, quantum physics demonstrates that no particle exists apart from its relationship with others. Take away the relationship, and there is no particle. There is nothing. This is true also with social existence. To say that life is relational is to acknowledge the vital interconnectedness not only of every particle, but of every person. Take away the community, and there is no person. What remains is an isolated individual. But to be human is to be in relationship.

The doctrine of God in Christianity—the Trinity—affirms the centrality of relationship. Theologians have traditionally distinguished between two ways of talking about God as the Three-in-One. The more accessible one is the "economic" theory that addresses how the one God is experienced in the process of salvation. The adjective is used here in its theological definition: the method of God's governance of and activity in the world. The other is called the "immanent" or "ontological" theory. It is the bold (some would say brash) attempt to address the mystery of the interior life of God. Whichever theological approach one takes to understanding the doctrine of the Trinity, the point here is that both are relational. The Christian's subjective experience of the one God—as Father, as Son, as Holy Spirit—is intimately personal. And to speak objectively of the mystery of whom God is as Three-in-One is to affirm that ultimate reality is personal and relational. In comparing the doctrine of the Trinity with the insights of quantum physics, Diarmuid O'Murchu states, "The doctrine of the Trinity is an attempted expression of the fact that the essential nature of God is about relatedness and the capacity to relate. The propensity and power to relate is, in fact, the very essence of God."[1]

An appreciation of relationships leads one to understanding faith not so much a matter of intellectually giving assent to a set of beliefs *about* God as it is personally trusting *in* God. This is illustrated in the theological doctrine of grace and works. The New Testament offers conflicting opinions regarding which is of greater importance. "By grace you have been saved through faith, and this is not your own doing ... not the result of works." [Ephesians 2:8-9] And elsewhere: "What good is it if you say you have faith but do not have works? Can faith save you? ... Faith by itself, if it has no works, is dead." [James 2:14-17] For centuries Protestants and Catholics were stereotyped by their emphasis upon one or the other. Happily, in recent years there has been an acknowledgement that both faith traditions share the same belief in this matter. We are saved by grace through faith; and faith without works is meaningless. In other words, we are saved through our relationship with the loving and just God, and this covenant relationship morally obligates us to our fellow human beings.

There is a parallel issue in organizing with relationships verses tasks. Relationships are primary. As an organizing principle states: *Take people where they are, not where you wish they were.* This is like grace. God accepts us as we are. But relationships are also purposeful. They make things happen. As another principle states: *Rewards go to people who do the work.* This is parallel to the biblical affirmation that faith without works is dead and ineffective. In organizing, relationships do not exist for their own sake. They are productive. They go somewhere.

Another way of looking at this tension between being and doing, between relationship-building and task-accomplishment, is a systems approach. There are basically two kinds of systems: familial and industrial. The former model is circular. As developed in psychotherapy, this model is illustrated by the family. It is primarily about relationships. What is the purpose of a family? What is its mission, its product? The purpose of a family is simply to be a family. The opening scene in the old film featuring Henry Fonda and Katharine Hepburn, "On Golden Pond," offers a playful picture of the family system. As they row across the pond to their cabin, they join in singing, over and over again, their silly but profound family litany to the tune of *Auld Lang Sein:* "We're here because we're here, because we're here, because we're here..."

But relationships must also bear fruit. The industrial model describes a system that has a product. The term is used here literally according to its Latin root, *industria,* meaning diligent activity directed to some purpose. It is linear, not circular. It is like a factory with raw ingredients coming in at one end of the assembly line and a finished product coming out of the other end.

The church is sometimes referred to as a "faith family." This circular model speaks to the primacy of relationships within the church. But there is more to a religious community of faith than this. It is not enough simply to care for itself and its own people. There is also a mission. Relationships are purposeful. They go somewhere. They must bear fruit.

Again this is illustrated by quantum mechanics as it describes how the fundamental building blocks of physical reality can be understood as either particles or energy. It all depends upon how the observer is looking at the data, and what one is looking for. It is not that one is true, and the other is not. Each accurately defines what is real from its perspective. Likewise with a congregation: it is simultaneously both a family of faith and a community of mission. It is constituted of relationships that go somewhere.

A priest who had been born and raised in Mexico and who serves a congregation north of the border tells of the striking difference he has observed in how houses are constructed. He spoke of how an excessively task-oriented process can kill the spirit. In Anglo culture the architectural plans are laid out and the individual workers promptly go after the task of building the house. But in Latino culture a group would first come together. They would talk about this and that. They would discuss, and maybe argue over, the design plans. But in the process they shared stories about their families. Relationships were being built first, and in the process the structure was built. It took a while, but when they were finished there was not only a building to show for their efforts, but a family to occupy it.

As with self-interest and power, relationships are also commonly defined in our society in ways that must be subjected to criticism. Popular culture emphasizes relationships as *quid pro quo* arrangements for meeting needs, whether for entering into sexual liaisons or for conducting business. In this distorted understanding relationships are primarily, if not exclusively, understood as emotional and utilitarian bonds. They are seen exclusively as the means to an end, a way to personal development and individual self-expression. Just as self-interest can be misunderstood as self-centeredness, so also relationships can be profoundly selfish.

Healthy relationships are, however, reciprocal. Whether in the family or in our employment, in church or in our organizing work with public officials, relationships must be of mutual benefit. Politicians sometimes complain, with good reason, that community organizations fail to reciprocate after receiving a pledge of support from them. The life-blood of every politician is the tangible support given that enables one to continue in office. It comes down to a matter of giving public affirmation to officials for their specific actions that have been helpful so that they receive credit. It's how political capital is acquired. I prefer not to use the term *quid pro quo* to refer to this process, since that conjures up negative associations with the buying and selling of votes. But reciprocity in relationship is key to the political process. As the organizing principle states, *relationships are reciprocal.*

The primacy of relationship in organizing is manifested in the one-to-one. This act of meeting with another person, and actively listening in order to discern the other's self-interest, is the foundational work upon which all community organizing is built. On the basis of what is learned in one-to-ones, issues are identified. Strategies are developed. Actions are conducted. And then the cycle is repeated, returning to doing one-to-ones. Moving along in the organizing process there can sometimes be a loss of energy or focus. What is it we are trying to accomplish? How do we renew our power? As the organizing principle affirms: *When in doubt, do a one-to-one.*

It is only in relationship that one can challenge others to clarify their self-interest and to hold them accountable. And it is only in relationship that others can hold us accountable. Relationships can be understood as the intersection of separate self-interests. Personal responsibility—being accountable—depends upon relationships. This accountability begins internally with the development of leaders. It then extends outward as the community organization holds public officials accountable.

In faith-based community organizing, relationships are purposeful. The fundamental goal is not to promote any particular political agenda nor even to address any particular issue. Rather, it is to develop an organization with the power of relationships that can act to make the larger community a more human place for all. An organizing principle: *organizing is about people; people are about issues.* Even when a particular organizing action does not meet all its objectives in moving an issue, it can still be considered a success. And that is because the primary goal is not to win, but to build a powerful organization.

Placing a priority on relationships would appear to emphasize *being* over *doing.* And yet surely this is a false dichotomy. Relationships that are unproductive—that have nothing purposeful to show for them—don't go anywhere. In community organizing the focus is kept on the purpose, rather than on the development of relationships for their own sake. As the organizing principle states: *No permanent allies, no permanent enemies, only permanent interest.*

Every real relationship involves conflict. Because every person, and every organization, is unique, there is no way to come together around common purposes without bumping up against each other. There is no way to reach agreement about shared interests without confronting different interests. Avoidance of conflict prevents the development of a relationship that is real and has power. Agitation is a key component of community organizing. Because the term "conflict" so often bears negative connotations in popular culture, organizing tends rather to speak of "tension." Another principle: *Change always involves tension.* And correspondingly: *Challenge is critical in a relationship.* A priority on relationship necessarily involves tension and challenge.

One of the frustrations in building a community organization is the discovery that some, perhaps most, of the religious congregations in a given city or locale choose not to participate. It comes down to a matter of self-interest. Some congregations and their pastoral leaders fail to see how working in partnership with others will be in their interests. Sometimes this is a consequence of a lack of imagination on the part of clergy leaders. But oftentimes it is for theological reasons. If a church is religiously exclusive, convinced that it has a monopoly on the truth, there is little incentive to work in partnership with those of other beliefs and faiths. Indeed, such cooperation could be seen as compromising one's beliefs and even contaminating one's spiritual purity.

The emphasis upon relationships in community organizing implies the necessity of listening to one another. The listening that is central to organizing affirms that the other person, whatever one's faith or lack thereof, embodies truth. True listening always risks our being changed by the other. It leads us to find a common ground of concern for the larger community that we all share amidst the differences that we cherish and that constitute our integrity.

Churches and synagogues that become involved in community organizing, whatever their respective faiths and theologies and ethics, tend to be those that embrace and value pluralism. It is *not* about being conservative or liberal. It is about placing a value on active listening. Again it comes back to a priority on relationship. Jacques Dupuis, a Jesuit theologian who spent much of his ministry in the religiously diverse environment of India, argues that religious pluralism is not something to be grudgingly tolerated out of necessity, but is to be embraced as a gift from God. Speaking out of his own Catholic faith tradition, Dupuis affirms the uniqueness of Jesus Christ as a *relative* reality: not, however, in the relativistic sense in which "relative" is opposed to "absolute," but in the sense of "relationship." He demonstrates how diverse religious traditions are mutually complementary, and that a relationship of dynamic interaction between and among traditions results in mutual enrichment.[2]

This is what is manifested in faith-based community organizing. It constitutes one of the most diverse groups of people and religious organizations imaginable. It cuts across racial and ethnic divisions, social and economic classes, conservative and liberal political interests, and religious faith traditions. Protestant and Catholic, Jewish and Muslim, Unitarian and Spiritualist, Buddhist and Humanist—all come together in faith-based organizing, because relationships are considered by all to be essential.

+ + + + +

The church I served in San Bernardino decided to enter into a planning process. Instead of taking the easy way out by mailing surveys to conduct a needs assessment of the congregation, we designed a process based upon community organizing principles and methods. Our community organizer worked in partnership with our denominational leaders in training a corps of leaders in the congregation who would carry out this process. Leaders were trained in conducting one-to-ones, beginning with one another. This disciplined listening campaign, focused not upon promoting church programming but upon identifying the personal self-interests of others, was in turn carried out with members of the congregation. The process was repeated in a second phase with these trained leaders conducting one-to-ones on neighbors and public officials and businessmen and women. Altogether, over half of the congregation and a considerable number of persons in the larger community received a one-to-one visit.

The results were electrifying. New energy was released in the congregation. A great deal of information was collected, of course. But most importantly, relationships were established and deepened. Later that year the annual stewardship drive was more successful than ever. Why? The church leadership attributed it to the planning visitation that had occurred earlier when there had been no mention made of finances. The following year the congregation struggled with a highly controversial topic—defining its stance toward gay, lesbian, bisexual, and transgender persons. As with any change, there was tension. But instead of dividing the membership as it potentially could have, a decision was reached that bound the church together in new ways and made it stronger than ever. Why? Again, leaders attributed this to the one-to-ones that had been conducted as part of the planning process. And there were other positive developments in the life of the congregation as well, among them the strengthening of ties with neighbors and an occasional new member as a result.

As in any vital organization, the development of leadership is key to its ability to grow and accomplish its mission. It is commonplace to make assumptions about who the leaders are in an organization and then to select candidates from that limited pool. But in community organizing there is a different way of looking at leadership. Every person is a potential leader. Anyone willing to do the work can be trained to become a strong leader.

New leaders in the congregation emerged as a consequence of our employing community organizing methodology in the programs of the church. Persons who had not assumed leadership positions earlier became identified for key positions in the life of the church. Over half of the moderators, the chief lay officer, ended up coming from the ranks of those who had been actively involved in the organizing work of the congregation.

Grounded in a theology of the ministry of the laity, we say in my faith tradition that all the baptized—all the members—are the ministers. It is parallel to the organizing principle that *organizers train leaders, and leaders do organizing*. Likewise, in the church the minister trains leaders, and leaders do ministry.

As a pastor I came to understand ministry in terms of being an organizing pastor. This concept will be explored in more depth in Chapter 15. But suffice it for now to say that each of the multitude of tasks involved in parish ministry is seen through the lens of community organizing methodology. At the heart of this approach is an understanding that power is in the relationship. And that means letting the people know you love them.

I am also learning that personally, spiritually, the most important relationship for me to nurture is with God. Embarrassing as it is to admit, too often in my days of active ministry I felt I was too busy to pray. Hopefully by the time I hang it all up I will have discovered fully that the quality and purposefulness of all my relationships depends upon my relationship with the One who gives me life in this world and is my only hope in the next.

Chapter 13

VALUE-DRIVEN POLITICS

"Ho, everyone who thirsts, come to the waters;
and you that have no money, come, buy and eat!
Come, buy wine and milk without money and without price.
Why do you spend your money for that which is not bread,
and your labor for that which does not satisfy?"
[Isaiah 55:1-2a]

"Economics, as channeled by its popular avatars in media and politics, is the cosmology and the theodicy of our contemporary culture. More than religion itself, more than literature, more than cable television, it is economics that offers the dominant creation narrative of our society, depicting the relation of each of us to the universe we inhabit, the relation of human beings to God."
[Gordon Bigelow]

To speak of the centrality of relationships leads directly into the fourth foundational concept for faith-based community organizing—*VALUES.* Not only are relationships, as defined above, grounded in core values of religious faith and expressive of them. So also it can be said that values are relational.

All networks engaged in broad-based and faith-based organizing acknowledge that values are a dimension of the organizing process. Jose′ Carrasco, political scientist and veteran community organizer, argues that values are indispensable and should be understood not simply as one dimension but as central to community organizing. As he has taught in numerous training events, values are like an adhesive, a glue that holds everything together. An organizing principle derived from his own words: *Values and self-interests are two sides of the same coin.* Push someone long and hard enough about their interests, Carrasco says, and we learn their true values.[1]

Although not universally embraced among community organizers, this book argues what Jose′ Carrasco has especially emphasized, namely that there is one principle most basic of all: *organizing should always be value driven, and not issue driven.* Turning problems into tangible issues is essential to organizing. But issues change. They do not drive faith-based organizing. It is values that endure. Whenever any particular issue becomes the central purpose of the organizing activity, what is ultimately important will have been displaced by the fleeting cause of the moment.

In Richard Wood's analysis of democratic organizing in America, we are reminded that power in congregation, faith-based community organizing is derived from far more than our ability to organize people, run public meetings, and negotiate with political representatives and economic elites. The development of leaders who have the civic skills essential to engaging in public life is required, of course. But there is more. And that is the unique identity of being faith-based, with organizing centered in the values of participating religious congregations. In faith-based organizing, power ultimately comes from the ability to articulate "a moral vision of society." Such a vision provides "ethical leverage" in the organizing task. Real power, as Wood argues, comes from the infusion of organizing techniques with "moral-political meaning drawn from the incorporation of religious symbols, commitments, stories, and assumptions." [2]

A play written by Charlayne Woodard—*Flight*—powerfully enacts how values are discovered in and given voice through the telling of stories. This drama is actually a story filled with many stories and demonstrates the importance of telling stories. Set in a Georgia plantation in 1858, the stage is dominated by a huge tree. Although the audience never sees him nor hears him, there is a little boy hiding in the branches because his mother Sadie that very day had been sold off the plantation. Why? Because she had been teaching her son to read.

In an effort to coax Li'l Jim down from the tree, five persons from the plantation take turns telling him stories. But the story telling has deeper purposes. The adult community is obviously trying to console the young boy by telling him the same stories he had heard earlier from his mother. They are reassuring the boy that he is not alone in spite of his incredible loss. The medium is the message in the act of story telling, demonstrating that he is connected to a community and to a tradition reaching back over countless generations. In the community's response to his grief, Jim is given a new future. In other words, the fundamental values that give life meaning and purpose and hope are transmitted through the telling of these stories.

Every once in a while the tree shakes violently reminding us that the object of this story-telling is still there, listening and absorbing every word. The stories are funny and sad, profound and bitter, angry and hopeful. They all come out of the slaves' own experiences reaching back to their African origins. The title of the play comes from one especially gripping portrayal of evil. It tells of a young girl who, having just given birth, was unmercifully whipped when she paused in the field to nurse her infant. The story ends with her flying away over the fields.

Values, as the term is used in organizing, are articulated through vision. What is vision but a way of seeing—not only what is obviously out there, but seeing what should be and could become a way of shaping life together in human society? Values are the lenses through which we see from the heart.

"Where there is no vision, the people perish." [Proverbs 29:18] These familiar words from the Book of Proverbs, taken from the King James Bible in particular, remind us of the critical importance of articulating a vision. Without vision, not only do the people perish, but so also religious congregations and community organizations. The New English Bible translates these familiar words less eloquently, but with an intriguing twist of phrase. "Where there is no one in *authority,* the people break loose." Without vision/authority, community disintegrates.

It should be apparent that any activity describing itself as faith-based, especially one centered in the life of a religious congregation, would be based upon values. But as with each of the three other concepts discussed above, this term also is defined by organizers in nuanced and unique ways.

+ + + + +

Once again, it helps to begin by negative example to identify what faith-based organizing does *not* mean when it speaks of values.

Values in organizing are not the same as the partisan "framing" of issues in the language of values. Beginning about three decades ago, in the face of long being the minority party in Congress, Republicans became especially adept at identifying and appealing to the "values" of ordinary Americans: Family values. Traditional values. American values. The ability to articulate their political platform in terms of values had tremendous power, as witnessed by their success in recent elections. Not surprisingly, Democrats are now playing catch-up, learning how to speak the language of values and framing their partisan issues by an appeal to values. But these are more a reflection of market analysis than of the discernment of values as understood in organizing. Through focus groups and polls the hot-button feelings of persons interviewed are identified and then wrapped around a pre-existing ideology. This approach taken by both Democrats and Republicans is Machiavellian in its traditional understanding: the denial of morality in political affairs and the use of deceit in pursuing and maintaining political power. This is the very opposite of what is meant by values in faith-based community organizing.

Values are *not* the same as political ideology. Each person has his or her ideological biases—an understanding of how power in society should be organized. [3] There have been two major ideologies operative in American political and economic life: classical *laissez faire* liberalism, which today is ironically called conservatism; and reform, or progressive, liberalism. The former emphasizes a free marketplace with a minimum of interference and a minimal role for government in providing for the public arena. The latter sees a greater role for government in regulating the marketplace and in providing a "level playing field" to compensate for inequities in economic resources and opportunity. The former is, of course, primarily associated with Republicans, and the latter with Democrats—although there is considerable overlap of ideologies with many elected leaders. There are additional ideologies operative in American life today as well, although relatively minor in their impact: such as Marxism and libertarianism. Fascism is another, rarely openly acknowledged, but always a potential when the power of the state is unchecked by constitutional processes. It is important to know and appreciate the ideological lenses through which we primarily view the world and to see how others view the world. But values, as we speak of them in organizing, are more primal than ideology. They have more to do with heart than head.

Values are *not* the same as religious dogma or doctrine. As with "framing" and ideology, beliefs also have been confused with values. However else one might critique the administration's "faith-based initiative," this political strategy of the party in power suggests that the religious faith of congregations and the "values" identified through market research are one and the same. Each faith tradition has its doctrine—its teachings—and this informs the life of the congregation and spiritually forms those who belong to it. But values, as the term is used in organizing, are more personal and relational. The core values of a congregation obviously must be consistent with its official teachings. But it isn't so much that values are derived from doctrine as the other way around. Values precede doctrine as the spiritual impulse, the heart beat, informing our particular beliefs. It is like being in love. More important than what we know *about* our beloved is the experience we have *of* the one we love. This experience is real, but much more difficult to articulate. Hopefully there is a correlation between our objective knowledge and our experiential knowledge. But the realm of values, as the term is understood in faith-based organizing, is closer to the latter.

Jose´ Carrasco teaches that values are dormant and need to be "massaged, challenged and intellectually stimulated." He speaks of an "awakening of the spirit" that comes out of relationships. Values are expounded through the pain that a person is expressing. Self-interest is the desire to alleviate one's pain and is therefore a good window into one's values. The two-sided coin metaphor applies not only to self-interests and values, but also to power and relationships. As Carrasco says, power comes from "the breathing of life," and values emerge from this spiritual awakening.[4]

So, what are values? Literally, value has to do with worth. It is primarily an economic term referring to the amount, as of goods or services or money, considered to be a fair and suitable equivalent for something else. To speak of values as is done in community organizing prompts a person to ask questions about the way goods and services are distributed. It is often wrongly assumed that an economic system is an unchangeable aspect of reality, something simply given to us that is beyond human control. In fact, however, how a society organizes itself to distribute its wealth is a political decision. Economic systems are not instituted by God, but are important human inventions.

One way to understand values in our culture is to pay critical attention to television commercials. As stated earlier, values are embedded in story. The advertising industry knows this well. There is no better way to discern the values of our consumerist culture than to pay close attention to advertisements, both printed and video. Virtually every television ad is a mini-narrative. The advertising industry refers to the series of stills that condense an ad to state its message as a "*story* board."

Surely no one has escaped the "priceless" series of advertisements promoting MasterCard. Each ad begins with a list of stuff and a matching set of prices. Then comes a phrase identifying some intangible that can't be purchased. A typical ad goes something like this: luggage for the trip, $125; new traveling outfit, $250; airline tickets to Paris, $800 each; springtime in Paris with your spouse-lover-partner, PRICELESS. Then comes the concluding assertion: "There are some things money can't buy. For everything else, there's MasterCard."

The genius of these ads is that they appeal to our idealistic impulses while selling us stuff that costs a lot of money. We know in our heart of hearts how empty materialism is and that meaningful relationships are not in fact a commodity available for purchase. Nevertheless, the devious attraction of these ads is that you can't get to the "priceless" moment without shelling out a pile of dough, or more accurately, without going into a mountain of debt.[4]

What is that old definition of a cynic? Someone who knows the price of everything, and the value of nothing. The prophetic witness offers another vision. "Come, buy wine and milk without money and without price. Why do you spend your money for that which is not bread, and your labor for that which does not satisfy?" [Isaiah 55:1-2a]

Faith-based organizing is value driven. Values are embedded in stories. It is the clergy role, as steward of the values, to have a critical awareness of the stories of the consumerist world in which our people live, and to know by heart the stories of our people, and to set these stories in the larger context of the story of God which in truth expresses the only value that is "priceless."

Value is, therefore, a highly personal matter. It is the worth in usefulness or importance to the possessor. It comes from a Latin term meaning "to be strong." The root lying behind the word is related to governance and power. And worth gives us the word "worship" pointing more to what we value, give worth to, than to what ideas we hold.

In other words, as Jose′ Carrasco has taught, values arise from self-interest. They are manifested in the pain that people are expressing. And personal/family pain is always linked with one's self-interest. That is why we listen so diligently to the stories others have to tell, paying more attention to the heart than to the head, to the feelings expressed even more than to the words being spoken. Stories express a person's concerns, fears, angers, and passions. This is the window into one's self-interest that points at the same time to one's values—what a person gives worth to.

We say in organizing that one should have *no permanent allies, and no permanent enemies*. This ordinarily refers to how the organization externally relates to the political process in the public sphere. This is why, as veteran community organizer Jim Keddy recommends, we should be "ideologically agile." Our understanding of values precedes political ideologies and partisan agendas. In this sense, values are neither conservative nor liberal.

But this organizing principle relates to the internal life of an organizing congregation as well. How else could persons of different religions ever work together when our faith traditions hold such conflicting positions on so many matters related to ecclesiology, dogma, ethics, and faith itself? The path to working together is through identifying the values we hold in common. As Americans we share democratic values, or as Richard Wood puts it, values of "ethical democracy." As people of faith we share religious values, appealing especially to the prophetic tradition of justice-love that is ubiquitous in the Jewish and Christian Bibles. And what is most important of all to tap are the personal values that lie deep within the human soul as each of us struggles to live with dignity and hope.

It takes little imagination to consider the many points at which faith-based organizing work could flounder. It is not necessary even to mention them; every pastor knows what the divisive issues are. Without denying differences, religious leaders build upon the values arising from the human heart—the flip side of the self-interest coin—shared values that undergird each of our separate religious witnesses. The Latin root points to values that are shared: *religio,* meaning "to bind together." Not only does organizing require an ideological agility, but it could be argued that the religious life also calls for a certain agility. The term "*doctrinally* agile" certainly would not be useful or acceptable to any religious leader, given the seriousness with which each of us takes the unique beliefs of our respective traditions and the teaching role of the clergy. But those who work side-by-side in faith-based organizing are very flexible—open and accepting, justice-loving and God-fearing. Perhaps we could say of persons engaged in faith-based community organizing that one is "*spiritually* agile." In the face of inflexible fundamentalism and polarizing partisanship, faith-based organizing by contrast is distinguished by agile spirits!

The challenge of faith-based organizing is to identify narratives of hope for today, acknowledging that they do not all come from the Bible. Values are the seeds of hope, and those seeds need to be planted whatever their source. The African myths and plantation stories told by Charlayne Woodard point to one source of values in the midst of this broken world that powerfully proclaim an open future.

Values are embedded in the personal stories of the families of our communities. In one-to-one visits with neighbors, we are not likely to learn what a person truly values by asking directly. The response would more likely be a list of moral abstractions. But ask a person to tell his or her story and values implicitly come tumbling out. "Let me tell you about the time we were sitting in the living room watching television and a bullet crashed through the window missing my little girl by an inch!" "When my son had a high fever we had to go to the emergency room because we have no insurance to pay for a doctor, and we had to wait all night long before anyone would even look at him!" "My friend was almost killed on her way to Bible study last week. She had to drive her wheel chair on the busy street because the city hasn't gotten around to cutting curb ramps in our neighborhood yet!" Stories such as these reveal self-interests, which also point to what is truly valued: life; security; home; family; children; health. And the list goes on and on. So, when the organizing congregations gather in an "action" to make their case before the public officials, the centerpiece is the testimony—personal stories told by the people of the community themselves. This is what drives the message home. And values drive the organizing.

People of faith turn also to the biblical story to express their most precious values. Walter Brueggemann writes of how the central values of the biblical faith tradition are in conflict with the values of our dominant culture today. These values are expressed through what he calls metanarrative—the larger story that holds together and gives expression to all the smaller stories that shape our lives. He identifies the central value system of our social context in the West today as military-consumerism. This narrative is powerful and compelling. This national/imperial story is the very air we breathe. It is so close to us that it is difficult to see.

In contrast there is the metanarrative of the Bible. It testifies to an alternative way of imagining life in the world. The testimony of the scriptures is that God invites us to live, right now in the midst of all that crushes life and violently destroys the good creation, in a transformed world marked by (a) undomesticated holiness, (b) "originary" generosity, (c) indefatigable possibility, (d) open-ended interaction, and (e) genuine neighborliness. In other words, in place of the violence and despair of the present rule of military-consumerism, faith means living by another story—the narrative of the reign of God that is manifested in justice-love, freedom, and hope.[5]

To be sure, there are sub-texts in the Bible that frequently draw more attention—such as God's command in Joshua [6:21] to kill all the women and children already occupying the land promised to ancient Israel, or the religious exclusiveness of the Gospel of John [7:1] that condemns Jews as the killers of Christ. But these stories, embarrassing and regrettable and shameful, are subordinate in the larger narrative of the Bible. As with every family story, it is the responsibility of the reader to face the skeletons in one's closet and to discern the themes that are of lasting value.

This is what Martin Luther King Jr. in 1962 so powerfully expressed on the steps of the Lincoln Memorial in his "I have a dream" speech. It was nothing less than a sermon that captured the imaginations of Americans across the racial divide. He basically told the American story, in its ugly reality and in its beautiful possibilities. The power of a story is that it is open-ended. Values open the door to a new future.

Through powerful metaphors dear to every American—fairness, security, freedom, equality, dignity, discipline—the Reverend Dr. Martin Luther King Jr. tapped into an ocean of shared values. In the middle of his speech he introduced an image that touched raw nerve endings across the land—a bounced check. These words are less often quoted as the nation annually observes his birthday. And yet, in a capitalist society, there is nothing more challenging, or more threatening, than to speak of values with such literal forcefulness. What is life worth? King translated the most complex and bewildering reality of economic injustice into terms that everyone, from the richest to the poorest, can grasp: "America has given the Negro people a bad check which has come back marked 'insufficient funds'. But we refuse to believe that the bank of justice is bankrupt. ... So we have come to cash this check..."

Martin Luther King's dream expressed the core values of our nation that lie close to every American heart. These values speak of the day when "all of God's children, black men and white men, Jews and Gentiles, Protestants and Catholics, will be able to join hands and sing in the words of the old Negro spiritual, 'Free at last! Free at last! Thank God Almighty, we are free at last!'"

\+ \+ \+ \+ \+

I am confident that I was finally beginning to figure out how to be a pastor when it came time for me to retire. Coming to understand values as foundational to doctrine as well as to ethics made me, I think, a better preacher. I came to realize that my primary task was not to convince people how to think correctly about theology or to straighten them out about their politics. God knows that I tried to do both more than once over the years! No, my primary task was relational, appealing to the values we shared. Most important of all was that I stand with the people entrusted to my pastoral care, my self with its interests alongside the other selves each with their interests. Our success in communicating as religious leaders, after all, comes down to a matter of being able to touch that center of value for the person in the pew.

Personally, as I seek to be ideologically and spiritually agile, I think I am, by the grace of God, becoming a better son and brother and husband and father and grandfather and friend. At least I hope so. I am quite sure that my focus upon values—rather than on political ideology and religious doctrines—is helping me to relate more effectively to the diverse members of my far-flung family. Many in the family are secular with no religious loyalties. Some are intentionally spiritual but avoid affiliation with or participation in any religious institution. There is a diversity of sexual orientation. Some in the larger family are very conservative, politically and religiously, although most are liberal.

What is it that holds families together? It is telling stories, listening to one another, and expressing love and respect and acceptance. Families, as with all manifestations of human community, are finally bound together by shared values, affirming the unique gifts—the self-interests—of each member.

The ultimate expression of values occurs in prayer. What is prayer, after all, than disciplined listening to discern God's self-interest? I would like to think that my morning spiritual exercises have been enriched by focusing upon values, upon that which alone is ultimately of worth. Otherwise, I wouldn't have a prayer.

Summary of the Four Foundational Concepts

We began Part II with a graphic illustration of energy. Surrounded by a swirling interaction of elements, faith-based community organizing lives dynamically at the center.

Self-Interest, Power, Relationships, and Values: Each part is in relationship with the others. Take away one, and the entire force-field collapses. Fused together they create the highly energized, even explosive, activity known as faith-based community organizing.

Self-Interest and Values are not opposites, but are two poles of one orbit. So also are Power and Relationships.

Self-Interest and Values are two dimensions of the same reality—two ways of looking at the same thing. They cannot be separated without demonizing the former and trivializing the latter. To discern a person's self-interest is to know what they value. And to discern someone's values is to know their self-interest.

Power and Relationship likewise are held together in one orbit. Power is in the relationship. Relationship is power. Power apart from relationship lacks accountability and is therefore demonic. Relationship without power is ineffectual, leaving the illusion of intimacy without responsibility.

As part of the same systemic force field, each foundational concept is likewise dynamically related to those on the complementary orbit. Beginning with Self-Interest and moving counter-clockwise…

Self-Interest—Relationships: Self-Interest is an essential component of living in community, of being able to give to others. As moral social beings holding self-interests, our humanity is discovered in a community of self-interests.

Relationships—Values: Existence is relational. Nothing of value exists outside of a relationship.

Values—Power: Values are powerful. In providing center, direction, and motivation, values drive existence. Power must be grounded in values to be transformative for human community.

Power—Self-Interest: Self-Interest is the very center of power, the ability to act. To be a self-actualized person—in our congregations, our organizations, and in our own personal lives—is to be powerful.

Faith-based community organizing lives at the center of this force field. Every dimension of organizing—in the larger community, in the congregation, in the life of the organizing pastor—is energized by this dynamic interaction of Self-Interest, Power, Relationships, and Values. We turn now to examine one significant place where month after month this energy is released: the clergy caucus.

Chapter 14

JESUS' ORGANIZING STRATEGY:
A Clergy Caucus Reflection

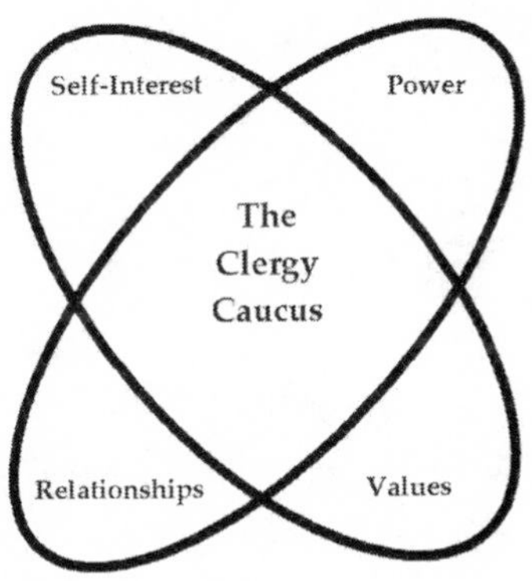

"Jesus was a community organizer. Pontius Pilate was a governor."
[A partisan slogan; nevertheless, up to a point at least, a truism.]

"What embitters the world is not excess of criticism, but an absence of self-criticism."
[G. K. Chesterton]

In the heat of the 2008 campaign, the Democratic candidate for president was attacked for having been a community organizer at an earlier point of his life. The Republican candidate for vice president bringing the charges was a state governor. It was only a matter of time—a few hours—before the above retort about Jesus and Pilate was widely disseminated. Suddenly, it seemed, this partisan slogan employing Christendom's most powerful religious symbols widely showed up on the bumpers of

America's automobiles.[1]

Was this a misuse of religious symbols? Probably. Identifying one candidate with the Son of God, and the other with his executioner, might indeed be considered over the top. And yet, to borrow from the title of a book reflecting on a much earlier political campaign, all's fair in love and war and running for president.[2]

Partisan campaign talking points aside, Barack Obama once was in fact a community organizer. He worked in a faith-based project of the Gamaliel organizing network. Obama tells of this experience in his autobiography, *Dreams From My Father*. Although he started out as an organizer without any particular religious affiliation, it was through his intimate exposure to the congregations in Chicago that he found a church and came to consider himself a person of faith.[3]

Obama's campaign and the first years of his presidency give evidence of his early experience as a community organizer. Attention to building a grassroots organization, emphasizing the power of relationships, pragmatically seeking middle ground, eschewing ideology, comfortably drawing upon religious symbols and personal faith—all these are signs of the influence of his once having been an organizer. This community organizing orientation served Obama well during his campaign but possibly is a weakness now that he has been elected and must govern. There should be no illusion about which role he came to play of the two contrasted on the bumper sticker. As head of the greatest empire ever to exist in the history of the world, President Obama is now a governor—big time!

Aside from partisan arguments, there is a degree of truth in the little saying about Jesus and Pilate. To begin with the latter, Pontius Pilate unquestionably was governor of the Judaea Province of the Roman Empire between 26-36 CE. The claim regarding Jesus requires some interpretation, however, since community organizing as we know it today is a modern phenomenon.

Jesus—as well as Moses, Joshua, Nehemiah, Paul and a host of other biblical characters—exemplified in their leadership styles the qualities associated with community organizers. Their power came from relationship. They listened to the pain that people were experiencing, developed leaders, and articulated a vision. Through this process they each built powerful organizations from the ground up that carried on their mission long after they died.

Jesus, in particular, is cited here as one who employed community organizing strategy and tactics. The general public in the first century, including Jesus and his followers, had little recourse to political decision-making. They were ordinary folk—not privileged, and certainly not of the ruling class. And yet, within decades there was in place an organization with a vision that turned the Roman Empire upside down. Practically speaking, from where did the church's power come in those years when it was persecuted and before it became established? What is the explanation for the Christian faith community's ability to act and so dramatically impact upon the public arena in those first three centuries?

Historians have attempted to account for this phenomenon in many ways. One especially convincing argument to explain this historical reality is made by Richard Horsley and Neil Silberman. Their hypothesis is that Jesus, and those who followed him, directly addressed the painful specifics of peasant life under the rule of Rome and its puppets. Far more than offering his listeners generalized promises or threats, he showed them that they were not condemned to be powerless victims. "This was not political protest in the sense of making overt, anti-government speeches or secretly plotting armed rebellion, but it was political in a far more powerful way. In Jesus' presence or under his influence, people who had been previously paralyzed or crippled by forces beyond their control began to piece their lives back together, for he offered them both a new feeling of community and a new personal confidence."[4]

In other words—and at the risk of grossly oversimplifying and trivializing the fullness of meaning that Christ holds for all who confess him to be the center of their faith—Jesus was a community organizer!

More thought needs to be given to this bumper sticker assertion, however. The most likely place in community organizing where such a claim is likely to be critically examined is the clergy caucus. Religious leaders serving congregations that participate in a faith-based organizing project in their local communities meet on a regular basis to reflect upon their shared ministries and political work. A term commonly used to refer to these meetings is clergy caucus. Not: ministerial association. Not: Bible study. Not: theological discussion group. But: clergy *caucus*. A caucus is a gathering whose purpose is action, not simply discussion. It is the self-interest of the participating clergy that is the primary agenda of these caucuses—providing peer support and nurture through prayerful reflection. But, as the name "caucus" implies, these are not mere support groups for pastors. Organizing staff—professional community organizers—also participate. The term "caucus" refers to an assembly devoted to political activity. The focus of these gatherings is the political work of building human community, *reflecting theologically upon public life.* There might be brief notices given at the caucus by the community organizer providing updates on what is going on. But the main reason for clergy to gather is to think theologically about what they do. In meeting together to reflect upon community organizing from the perspective of the faith and values of their respective traditions, clergy peer relationships are strengthened and our political work is held accountable.

Reflections in these clergy caucuses are based upon a variety of sources that embody the values of one's faith tradition: official social teaching pronouncements from denominational leaders, rabbinic disputes in the Talmud, current theological writings. But the primary source is the Bible that is ritually read each week in the congregations. Not infrequently a clergy participant in a caucus will choose to lead a reflection based upon a passage of scripture that is scheduled to be read during worship in the near future. When a caucus contains a diversity of faith groups, care is taken to ensure that all participants can relate to and benefit from the reflection. For example, readings from the Hebrew prophets are frequently used as the source for a reflection when a caucus includes Jews and Unitarians and Catholics and Protestants. But on occasion when the emphasis is placed upon historical processes and not confessional differences, even a scripture reading from the New Testament can be a constructive source of reflection among clergy from diverse religious faith traditions.

What follows below is an example of one such reflection in a clergy caucus. The text—Luke 10:1-11, 17-20—was the Gospel reading one summer Sunday for a number of churches that follow the common ecumenical lectionary—Roman Catholic, Episcopal, Presbyterian, Lutheran, United Methodist, Disciples of Christ, United Church of Christ, and others. Taking the text seriously in its original context and applying it to the work shared by the participating clergy, this reflection based on a shared scriptural text considers how Jesus organized his mission.[5]

\+ + + + +

PUTTING FAITH INTO ACTION:
Jesus' Strategic Plan for Mission

This story of the commissioning of the seventy is one of three texts identified by many Jesus scholars as an authentic source for presenting a picture of the historical Jesus. [6] The story of

Jesus sending a group of disciples to go ahead of him appears three times in the Gospels. The original story that inspires the others is found in Mark 6:6b-13. Here only twelve disciples are sent out. The story appears again, with slight variations, in Luke 9:1-6. Finally, in Luke 10:1 ff.—the text under consideration in this reflection—the story is expanded from twelve who are sent out to seventy (or seventy-two—the manuscript evidence is evenly balanced between these two numbers).

John Dominic Crossan argues that these texts present us with a unique picture of the historical Jesus and his strategy for engaging in mission. It takes both an ideal, creative vision and a practical, social program to constitute a mission. MISSION = CREATIVE VISION & SOCIAL PROGRAM. In this story of the commissioning of the seventy, Jesus combines the two. [7]

A verse-by-verse reading of this text reveals Jesus' organizing strategy:

> v. 1 *The Lord appointed seventy others and sent them on ahead of him in pairs to every town and place where he himself intended to go.*

The point Luke is making is that this mission is growing in influence. What started with one person, Jesus, expands at first to twelve in the calling of the disciples. In this story of the commissioning of the seventy the number of persons engaged in the very same mission as Jesus and the twelve increases six-fold. By the time we come to Luke's second volume, the Acts of the Apostles, there are three thousand persons added to the ranks on the Day of Pentecost. [Acts 2:41] Only two chapters later, in response to the preaching of Peter and John, the believers numbered about five thousand. [4:4] And the process continues as Paul carried the mission beyond Jerusalem and Judea and Samaria to the ends of the earth as it was known in the far-reaching Roman Empire of the 1st century CE. One, 12, 70, 3000,

5000... Luke counts like a community organizer!

At the heart of mission is not merely addressing issues, but building an organization. That is what Luke is describing. This is an organization that is being built with a broad base of leaders, not a movement confined to a solitary charismatic leader. Jesus does not hang on to this mission as if he is the only person who can carry it out. That would have limited the impact of his influence, confining results to himself alone and to the relatively few places where he was able to go. What Jesus does, however, is to release the mission to others as he sends them on ahead to places where he himself intended to go, but presumably couldn't. And in sending persons out in pairs, two-by-two, this mission builds into it accountability. Isolated, solitary activists bent on doing their own thing need not apply; this mission carried out in partnership is about building community.

v. 2 *He said to them, "The harvest is plentiful, but the laborers are few; therefore ask the Lord of the harvest to send out laborers into his harvest."*

The need addressed by this mission is overwhelming. The "harvest" of human hurt is plentiful indeed. Even when one focuses close to home—thinking globally, acting locally—the problems faced by families in our cities are massive. Who does not feel small and insignificant when faced with this seemingly insurmountable challenge?

But the same metaphor also expresses a sense of urgency about this mission. When the crops are ripe, they must be reaped. Harvest season is always a time of great urgency. We do not have the luxury of waiting until tomorrow to begin to organize.

v. 3 *"Go on your way. See, I am sending you out like lambs into the midst of wolves."*

This plentiful harvest of human need is not so much a problem as it is an opportunity. As long as the challenge remains a problem, it is elusive—too complex and bewildering to address. Once a problem is turned into an issue, however, it becomes manageable and achievable. To think in terms of issues rather than problems is to be on our way already.

This mission is not for the faint-hearted. There will be considerable resistance to overcome. The families of our communities are like innocents when pitted against well-organized, moneyed, special interest groups who have so much power. Power means simply the ability to act. But there is more than one kind of power—more than one way effectively to act, to bring about change. In addition to the power of money there is the power of relationship. Those whom Jesus sends out on this mission are like lambs, armed with the power of relationship, confronting those who are like wolves and armed with the power of money. It is not without risk to be a lamb in the midst of wolves. Which is why it is essential that the lambs be well organized!

> v. 4 *"Carry no purse, no bag, no sandals; and greet no one on the road."*

There is a tendency to think that the more armor one carries into battle, the safer one is. And the more paraphernalia brought along on a vacation, the more enjoyable the trip will be. But Jesus counsels those embarking upon his mission to travel lightly, discovering that their strength lies in their vulnerability. This mission will be accomplished not by glossy brochures and high-tech presentations, but by unadorned personal stories told with conviction and passion.

Once on the way, it is important to stay focused upon the task at hand. There will be many temptations to be diverted from the mission. Singleness of purpose on the journey is essential for assuring safe arrival at the desired destination.

> vs. 5-6 *"Whatever house you enter, first say, 'Peace to this house!' And if anyone is there who shares in peace, your peace will rest on that person; but if not, it will return to you."*

This mission is profoundly personal. The pronouncement of peace in the first century was a common greeting used by persons meeting others. The foundation stone upon which all community organizing is built is the one-to-one. These are invitational in nature, not coercive. They are based upon listening to the concerns of others and are not driven by an agenda. In wishing peace to a house and all who dwell within it is to value that particular family, respecting and honoring what they express to be in their interests.

There is no guarantee that those who open the door of their home will respond positively to our well-intentioned greetings. Indeed, they might not even come to the door! Our witness to peace—to *shalom,* to the wholeness of justice-love—in our broken, sin-sick world will not and need not receive a 100% response. There is no minimum level of response that is either expected or required to validate this mission. In fact, Luke gives us no clue about the size of response that the seventy received. He only reports that they returned with joy.

> v. 7 *"Remain in the same house, eating and drinking whatever they provide, for the laborer deserves to be paid. Do not move about from house to house."*

This mission is not about providing charity. Rather, it is about releasing power that is latent. This mission is not about brokering power, rendering others indebted to us. Rather, it is about the power of standing alongside another that liberates. This mission is not top down, in which persons of superior strength and insight make others to become dependent upon them in the name of providing assistance.

No, this mission is based upon hospitality. It is not an occasional excursion to the other side of the tracks to help those considered by us to be less fortunate, quickly retreating to the safety of our privileged enclave. But it is one that requires of us that we remain in the same place to share life together—in a spirit of mutuality and partnership and collaboration.

> vs. 8-9 *"Whenever you enter a town and its people welcome you, eat what is set before you; cure the sick who are there, and say to them, 'The kingdom of God has come near to you.'"*

This mission is focused upon specific, tangible, measurable goals—such as eating with our neighbors and curing the sick that are in front of us and speaking words of hope. There is no place here for utopian generalizations, like "God's in his heaven, all's right with the world." Nor is there true comfort to be found in religious clichés that promise salvation for the soul while ignoring injuries to the body. This mission is not one more of those endless discussions in which do-gooders moan and groan, grumble and complain, parade and posture. Rather, there is something tangible to show for our efforts. There are concrete results. This is about taking action.

> vs. 10-11 *"But whenever you enter a town and they do not welcome you, go out into its streets and say, 'Even the dust of your town that clings to our feet, we wipe off in protest against you. Yet know this: the kingdom of God has come near.'"*

This mission is pragmatic with eyes always focused upon the desired objective. No time is wasted where response is not forthcoming. This mission does not allow itself to become dragged down by the persons who don't respond and who don't take responsibility. Rewards go to those who do the work. This mission builds upon strength, not allowing its energies to be sucked up by weakness. Precious, limited resources are invested where there is positive response.

Those persons who do not respond cannot invalidate the mission. Something bigger is going on here than our own social and political concerns. The fact of the matter is that the kingdom of God *has* come near. It is at hand, within reach, something we can taste and touch in the present moment, however fragmentary it might be. God's reign of justice-love is being manifested in the here and now as we engage in this mission.

What is central to this particular mission as Luke describes it throughout his gospel is the God of Jesus. The purpose of this mission that Jesus sends the seventy out upon is not to make each of his followers into a little Jesus. Rather, his disciples are commissioned to the very same ministry that Jesus himself was engaged in: *eating* with sinners and outcastes, *curing* the sick and broken-hearted, and *making hope real* by proclaiming the reachable reign of God. As Jesus is a leader, those who follow him become leaders as well.

> vs.17-20 *The seventy returned with joy, saying, "Lord, in your name even the demons submit to us!" He said to them, "I watched Satan fall from heaven like a flash of lightning. See, I have given you authority to tread on snakes and scorpions, and over all the power of the enemy; and nothing will hurt you. Nevertheless, do not rejoice at this, that the spirits submit to you, but rejoice that your names are written in heaven."*

How did the seventy feel when they returned home from their organizing journey? They returned with joy! This mission is rewarding, not depleting. There is no burnout here. Instead of wells drying up, there are fathomless reservoirs of hope and strength and energy. In this mission there is something larger and more profound going on than ordinary political pursuits.

This mythological talk of Satan falling from heaven, and of

treading upon snakes and scorpions, is a reminder that this mission is no mere activist agenda for an improved world, but an action of cosmic scale. Where real authority is discovered and true power is exercised, we need not fear the outcome of these endeavors. For a life invested in this mission of Jesus is given to nothing other than the work of God. And that is indeed reason to *rejoice!*

\+ + + + +

Admittedly, to claim that Jesus was a community organizer is indeed a partisan slogan and a gross oversimplification. Christ is the center of faith for the church that bears his name. He is confessed by Christians throughout the world in many ways: Son of God, Lord, Messiah, Son of Man, Incarnate Word become Flesh, Truly Divine, Truly Human, to name a few. One must be careful not to misuse symbols of ultimacy to promote partisan objectives.

What this clergy caucus reflection demonstrates, however, is that the historical process described by Luke in this story of the commissioning of the seventy is in fact similar to the methodology of community organizing. There are parallels that shed insight on the organizing principles of self-interest, power analysis, relationship building, and most importantly the values that drive this political work. In this sense, faith-based community organizing can be understood as employing a similar strategy as that used by Jesus to carry out his mission and to build a powerful organization.

Most importantly, reflecting together as clergy colleagues on the work shared in community organizing is energizing. Relationships among religious leaders are strengthened. As sacred symbols come alive in fresh, new ways organizing pastors discover the power residing in their ministerial vocations to be unleashed.

Chapter 15

TELLING OUR STORY IN A NEW WAY: The Organizing Pastor

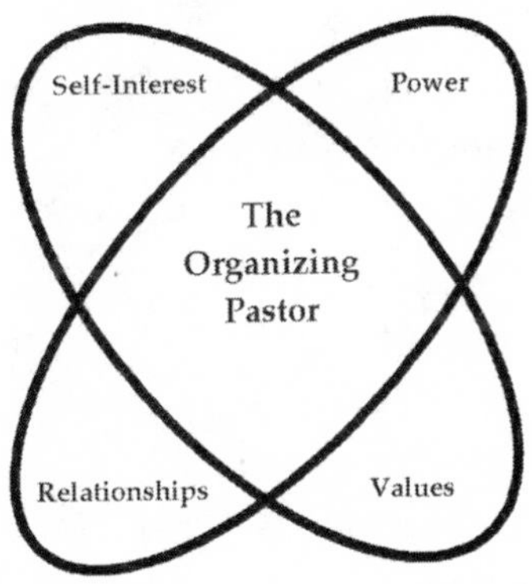

> *"Think of us in this way, as ... stewards of God's mysteries. Moreover, it is required of stewards that they be found trustworthy."* [First Corinthians 4:1-2]

> *"By and by, when the morning comes, when the saints of God are gathered home,*
> *We'll tell the story how we've overcome: for we'll understand it better by and by."*
> [Charles A. Tindley]

To be a religious leader engaged in community organizing is to be energized by the dynamic interplay of the four foundational concepts. Pastors have an essential role to play in community organizing that is faith-based. The question is: what precisely is that role, and how is it different from the leadership given by organizing staff and by lay leaders?

There are many models offered for understanding the traditional role of the religious leader. One that this author was taught in theological seminary decades ago was based upon three biblical metaphors: Prophet (inspired word: preaching & teaching), Priest (authentic worship: prayer & ritual), and King (faithful administration: service & organization). Integrity of the clergy office requires that all three be kept in balance. When one is emphasized at the expense of the others, there is distortion. The prophetic role by itself can lead to anarchy, the priestly role to clericalism, the kingly role to tyranny. But holding all three together in creative tension can result in a powerful office of leadership in religious congregation and democratic society.

In addition, my experience was that seminary students were invited to consider a particular focus for parish ministry. There are many aspects to the life of a pastor in a congregation. Among them are included preacher, teacher, sacramental minister, counselor, administrator, activist, and even program director. While the clergy role as a generalist in actuality involves all of these tasks, the challenge in being the religious leader of a congregation is to find a concept that unifies the diversity of expectations. One model, for example, that has been widely used over the past half century is the therapeutic, with specialized training offered in clinical pastoral education. A clergy leader could also operate from an academic model, seeing oneself primarily as a professor-teacher (a model especially appealing to the newly ordained after having spent several years in graduate school). Many clergy coming out of the tumultuous years of the Vietnam War and the civil rights movement took political activist as their model for being religious leader of a congregation.

Another model—that which is proposed here—is community organizing. To speak in terms of *the organizing pastor* is one way of understanding how the variety of clergy roles can be effectively integrated. A religious leader who has been trained in community organizing principles and methodologies is able to "organize" all the demands upon his or her time around the model of the organizing pastor.

What is central to being the religious leader of a congregation, whatever model one might operate from, is to be an interpreter of the core beliefs and values of the community of faith and its larger faith tradition. Faith-based community organizing that is understood as being driven by values especially emphasizes this. An organizing pastor's primary role in the life of the congregation in all of its various ministries is to be steward of the values. Or, because values are embedded in narrative, the religious leader is *steward of the stories.* [1] We turn now to a consideration of where one looks to discern the core values that drive the life of the congregation in all that it does, including its organizing work.

\+ + + + +

"Tell me your story." This is where faith begins—by listening to the stories of our families and congregations, and to stories from our religious traditions and the scriptures. What is the Bible but one big story linking together a host of little stories—a story of God in relationship with everything and everyone that God has created? Faith is a story of our listening to God, trusting that God is listening to us.

There is a story of the time a journalist interviewed Mother Teresa after she received the Nobel Peace Prize in 1979. He inquired what she asked God for when she prayed. "Nothing," she replied. "I just listen." "And what does God say to you?" the interviewer continued. "Nothing," Mother Teresa replied. "He listens."

That is where community organizing begins as well—by listening to the stories that have shaped a person's life. The one-to-one with which organizing begins and returns to over and over again is about paying attention to stories. And what is it that powerfully constitutes the heart and soul of every organizing action, but the passionate testimony expressed through personal stories of families in our communities.

As stated before, *organizing should always be value driven, and not issue driven.* This principle points to the human story that lies behind all organizing work. Because values are embedded in stories, we can also say that *faith-based community organizing is story driven.*

Each organizing network has its own story. The one this author is most familiar with is the PICO National Network. Co-founder and long-time executive director John Baumann, a Jesuit priest, tells of how PICO started off almost 40 years ago as a neighborhood-based organization. Although churches were encouraged to participate and provide support, at first they were kept at arm's length from the organizing activity. There was an attempt to keep the religious and political spheres separate. Some 15 years later an intentional decision was made to move from a neighborhood-based model to one centered primarily in the life of religious congregations. That led inevitably to being faith-based. This new approach of necessity emphasizes the importance of values. In addition to secular values recognized earlier that lie at the heart of our democratic society, organizing based in faith especially emphasizes those prophetic values arising from the biblical faith tradition. Organizing in the religious community is not only about the promotion of tolerance and civic participation, as essential as these values are, but is about working for a more just social order. Faith-based organizing is devoted to the prophetic vision to "let justice roll down like waters, and righteousness like an ever-flowing stream." [Amos 5:24]

It follows, then, that clergy have a particularly important role in the faith-based model of community organizing. Pastors and rabbis and other professional leaders of congregations are charged with the responsibility to be teachers and celebrators of the core values lying at the heart of their respective religious faith traditions. The integrity, growth and success of community organizing claiming to be "faith-based" depend upon the active participation of religious leadership. It is the role of clergy to ensure that religious symbols are not being manipulated to bless political agendas, and that organizing is value-driven in fact and not in name only.

Some organizing projects consider themselves to be "broad-based" rather than "faith-based." This refers to alliances made up of diverse groups such as labor unions and teacher associations and nonprofit agencies, as well as religious congregations. There are advantages as well as disadvantages to this approach. The broad-based approach to organizing has much in common with that which is faith-based with respect to principles and methodologies – such as self-interest, power analysis, leadership development, etc. In broad-based organizing clergy are recognized as "institutional leaders" along with the heads of unions and nonprofits who also are gatekeepers of their respective organizations. Values embedded in the stories of labor and education and religion are referred to, but what is especially emphasized are those shared by all in democratic society. The Bible, although centrally important for communities of faith, is not necessarily widely used as an explicit source for informing values in broad-based organizing. And with religious congregations constituting only one of several kinds of institutions participating in broad-based organizing, prayer tends not to be part of training and assemblies and actions.

In faith-based organizing, however, clergy are considerably more than the gatekeepers of their respective institutions. Far more importantly religious leaders are recognized as being responsible for grounding the life of the congregation, including outreach to the larger community, in the teachings of their respective faith traditions. So also clergy are responsible for creating an environment in which each participating member is valued.

Paul, in claiming to be an apostle, referred to himself as "a steward of God's mysteries" rather than a promoter of his own doctrine. [First Corinthians 4:1ff.] "Mystery" comes close to what is meant in faith-based organizing when speaking of values. Religious leaders might consider themselves to be stewards of the congregation's values, discerning the self-interests of member families and ensuring that each person entrusted to their care is listened to and affirmed as a child of God.

This mystery that constitutes values is told through story. That is what lies at the heart of liturgy—the telling and enactment of the sacred story. It is done through prayer and offering, through preaching and sacrament. Kevin Bradt reflects about how stories are mysterious, pointing the way to a reality that is open, unknown, indeterminate, irreducible, rich with meaning that cannot be nailed down and contained by any single interpretation. "Mystery," Bradt writes, "invites inquiry rather than definition, erotic participation rather than geometric proof, relationship rather than reason, pursuit rather than purchase."[2]

In other words, mystery sounds a lot like story. As stewards of God's mysteries, of the congregation's values, religious leaders are called to be stewards of the people's stories.

Gospel hymns speak powerfully to the place of story in articulating pain and possibility. In the early 20th century the famous Methodist preacher, Charles Albert Tindley, wrote many hymns. One of them, "I Shall Overcome," is widely considered to be the source of the adaptation that subsequently became the theme song of the civil rights movement. But it is another that develops in depth the theme of poverty and destitution. The promise of a new and better future comes not from denial or avoidance of the suffering in the present time, but naming it.

We are often tossed and driven on the restless sea of time;
Somber skies and howling tempests oft succeed a bright sunshine…

We are often destitute of the things that life demands,
Want of food and want of shelter, thirsty hills and barren lands…
Temptations, hidden snares often take us unawares,
And our hearts are made to bleed for many a thoughtless word or deed…

The theological message of this evangelical hymn is the very opposite of the old adage about an escapist kind of religion so heaven-bound that it is of no earthly good. Hope that is real, having the power to sustain persons caught in the bewildering snares of poverty, is grounded in the story of struggling to survive in the face of injustice. As the song concludes in its powerful refrain:

By and by, when the morning comes,
When the saints of God are gathered home,
We'll tell the story how we've overcome:
For we'll understand it better by and by.

The task of an organizing pastor is essentially the same as that which the Rev. Dr. Martin Luther King did so eloquently and so powerfully in his "I Have a Dream" sermon-speech. This is not in the sense necessarily of having the same charisma, as welcome as that would be. But it is to affirm that all the activity of the congregation, including community organizing, is grounded in the symbols of faith. Pastor Martin Luther King Jr. is a model for the organizing pastor, not in his top-down, masculinist leadership style, but in his genius for grasping and articulating the symbols of faith. The pastor's role, as Dr. King excelled in, is to listen to the story—the American story, the biblical story, the human story of persons longing for a new future—and then to tell this powerful story, and to tell it powerfully.

As an old Sunday School hymn affirms: "I love to tell the

story, for those who know it best / seem hungering and thirsting to hear it, like the rest. / And when I sing in glory, I know the new, new song / will be the old, old story that I have loved so long."

This is the primary job of one who understands the role of the clergy as organizing pastor. Religious leaders speak from their own particular religious faith tradition. They tell the "old, old story" of God's steadfast love. It is a story of justice that is distributive, not retributive. Embedded within this story are the values that drive the organizing work. Our families, our communities, our nation are hungering and thirsting for a story that will empower an alternative reality. What we yearn for is a story that will open the future. What our hearts ache for is a narrative that gives us hope.

\+ + + + +

The religious leader of a congregation who intentionally chooses the model of the organizing pastor—rather than, for example, that of pastoral counselor or political activist—finds that all the dimensions of the clergy role are focused by the discipline of community organizing. Pastoral care is shaped by listening to stories and helping persons to recognize their self-interests and the values that lie behind them. Preaching and the leadership of worship seek to find connections between the stories of the congregation and the larger redemptive story of the faith tradition. Administration is understood as the story of building community, discerning mission, and organizing to accomplish the congregation's mission.

The primary responsibility of the organizing pastor is the life of the congregation. While it is the professional community organizer's job to build a powerful community organization called a federation, it is the pastor's job to build a powerful organization called a congregation.

The pastor's main role with the community organizing outreach activity of the congregation is ensuring that this political work is grounded in its values. One important way in which this is done is through participating in the congregation's committee/ministry team that is entrusted with the community organizing work of the congregation. Sometimes called a Local Organizing Committee (LOC), this ministry meets regularly to receive reports of one-to-ones that have been conducted, to receive training from the professional organizer assigned to the congregation, to conduct research, to plan next steps. There are many ways the pastor can contribute to the work of the LOC—providing perspective on the culture of the congregation, helping to identify persons who could be invited to participate, and providing moral support simply through being present and interested. But the essential task of the organizing pastor in the LOC is to be steward of the values. When the clergy leader gives a reflection at each meeting connecting the organizing work with the beliefs and core values of the congregation, prayerfully reflecting upon the scriptural stories that are to be read in worship in the weeks ahead, leaders become powerfully equipped to engage in ministry and mission.

While the primary role of the organizing pastor is to build a powerful moral community called a congregation, clergy also have a public role in our society. Religious leaders symbolize by their office the values of the ethical community aspired to in American society. In faith-based organizing, pastors—ministers, priests, rabbis, imams, sisters, deacons—are called upon to give leadership beyond the congregation in the work of the larger community organization—e.g., by offering a prayer at an action, or by assisting in a research meeting, or by serving on the board of the federation. While clergy bring many gifts to this public activity, their most important function is symbolic—representing and articulating the values that are essential to the building of a just social community.

Richard Wood speaks of a symbiotic relationship between religious congregations and the organizing federation, between clergy leadership and professional community organizers. In this relationship, each specializes in particular tasks and orientations. There is a symbiotic relationship between the pastor of a congregation and the community organizer who is responsible for the federation. To speak of symbiosis is to acknowledge the mutual dependence of one upon the other to thrive and grow. Clergy need the expertise of community organizers to make their congregations effective in building a world that manifests the values lying at the heart of human community. And organizers need congregations and clergy to provide leadership that is essential to doing the relationship building and research and actions. At the heart of both interrelated endeavors is an ethical vision of what constitutes a just human community. "The ultimate task for both lies in using the moral-political traditions of religion to guide immediate political efficacy and congregational development, in order to generate dynamic, ethically rooted democratic engagement over the long term."[3]

Faith-based organizing takes seriously the mandate expressed by Martin Luther King Jr. that the religious community has a unique role in enhancing democracy and helping to shape a more just society. Acknowledging its many faults, he calls for the church to be the "chief moral guardian of the community." [4] Rather than be the timid reflection of the status quo and a comfortable ally of privilege, the faith community must "recapture its prophetic zeal" and rekindle human imagination. Religious congregations and their leaders have a unique civic role distinguishing them from the agencies of government as well as from other institutions in society. "The church must be reminded that it is not the master or the servant of the state, but rather the conscience of the state. It must be the guide and the critic of the state, and never its tool."[5]

The religious leader is far more than gatekeeper of an institution. He or she is steward of the values of the congregation—values that are embedded in the stories of the men, women, and children who constitute it and of the larger faith story that is recalled and celebrated each week. It is important to ensure that every dimension of the life of the congregation, including its community organizing work, is truly value-driven. Also, in partnership with other religious leaders and organizers, the pastor's role is to be one of the stewards of the values of the larger community.

It is not only community organizing that is value-driven. Democracy, too, must be value-driven. The enhancement of democracy in America is dependent upon values of justice and love. Someone has got to be in the driver's seat when it comes to values. Clergy can and must take turns at the wheel, sharing the responsibility with strong leaders and organizers to ensure that voices of ordinary families are heard in the public square. But when nighttime descends and the ride continues into the dark of human hurt and longings, clergy know that they cannot afford to sleep. It is then time to stay awake and to take our turn behind the wheel.

Conclusion

WRITE THE VISION AND MAKE IT PLAIN

The question was raised at the beginning of this book about mixing religion and politics—not whether, but how? In democratic America they always have been mixed, and always will be.

It has been acknowledged that some efforts to mix the two are not healthy for either religion or politics. But it can be done. The argument of this book is that the most effective way the two can be mixed constructively is through the radical democracy of faith-based community organizing.

Religious congregations have much to contribute to the health of our democracy. Giving voice to ordinary families, holding public officials accountable, helping to shape public policy reflecting core values of our nation—all these are important. But no task is more crucial than that of articulating a moral vision of what America can become.

Late in the 7th century BCE, with the biblical faith community in crisis as the sole remaining vestige of the once proud Davidic empire was dying by inches from threats internal and external, a prophet by the name of Habakkuk was bold to speak a word on behalf of God. "Write the vision; make it plain on tablets, so that a runner may read it. For there is still a vision for the appointed time; it speaks of the end, and does not lie. If it seems to tarry, wait for it; it will surely come, it will not delay." [Habakkuk 2:2-3]

What is pictured here is a sign with lettering so large that a runner can read it while racing by. Today it would be a huge billboard with a message so clear that it could be seen above all the others competing for our attention as one speeds along on the freeway. It is a vision so commanding that it captures the attention and invites the passionate response of persons hungry for hope.

This is what happens when faith storms the public square through community organizing. This political work is driven by values. It is a new way of seeing. It is a new way of envisioning. This new way of mixing religion and politics storms into the future with a vision of a democratic America that is nothing less than seeing from the heart.

ENDNOTES

Chapter 1: DEMOCRACY IN ACTION

1 This conversation will be revisited in Chapter 10 where the topic of self-interest is explored in depth.

2 See a recently published book by political scientist Heidi J. Swarts for a comprehensive and up to date analysis of community organizing in America today: *Organizing Urban America: Secular and Faith-based Progressive Movements* (Minneapolis: The University of Minnesota Press, 2008). Swarts compares and contrasts two fundamentally different approaches to community organizing: the secular and more individualized basis as found in ACORN on the one hand, with the institution-based or faith-based as found in IAF, PICO, DART, and Gamaliel on the other hand. Each approach assumes a different "mobilizing culture," and each approach has its strengths and weaknesses in effecting social change. Swarts' book is an excellent overview of the variety of ways in which Alinsky-informed organizing is carried out today, including the secular approach of ACORN. As the title of my book implies, however, all attention is given to that approach that Swarts refers to in shorthand as CBCO – Congregation Based Community Organizing.

Chapter 2: MIXING RELIGION AND POLITICS

1 The claim that religion and politics have been mixed throughout our nation's history will be documented in subsequent chapters. This is a central thesis of Alexis de Tocqueville's classic study of democracy in America cited in chapter 3, as well as Andrew Delbanco's imaginative "meditation on hope" inspired by Tocqueville's thought. In chapters 6 & 7 in particular the interweaving of religion and politics is documented as integral to our nation's original

stories.

2 Dennis A. Jacobsen, *Doing Justice: Congregations and Community Organizing* (Minneapolis: Fortress Press, 2001), 27. Although there are a growing number of excellent books on community organizing, most are written from a sociological or political science perspective, including professional community organizers themselves. Relatively little has been written from a religious perspective. Jacobsen's book is a notable exception. Some others include: Gregory F. Augustine Pierce, a Catholic priest and organizer, who wrote *Activism That Makes Sense: Congregations and Community Organization* (Chicago: ACTA Publications, 1984). Two examples by Robert C. Linthicum, who has written extensively on urban ministry, are *Empowering the Poor: Community Organizing among the city's 'rag, tag and bobtail'* (Monrovia, CA: MARC Publishing, 1991) and *Building a People of Power: Equipping Churches to Transform Their Communities* (Colorado Springs, CO: Authentic Publishing, 2005). But Jacobsen's book is among the few, to my understanding, that has reflected theologically upon organizing strategy and methodology as applied to the particular faith-based setting of religious congregations.

3 Heidi Neumark, *Breathing Space: A Spiritual Journey in the South Bronx* (Boston: Beacon Press, 2003).

4 Early in his second year as President of the United States, Thomas Jefferson responded to a letter of concern from the Danbury Baptist Association in Connecticut: "...I contemplate with sovereign reverence that act of the whole American people which declared that *their* legislature should make no law respecting an establishment of religion, or prohibiting the free exercise thereof, thus building a wall of separation between church and state." [Library of Congress]

Chapter 3: DEMOCRACY UNDER SIEGE

1 Alexis de Tocqueville, *Democracy in America,* trans. Arthur Goldhammer (New York: Library Classics, 2004).

2 The following are only a few who have expressed concerns about the future of our democracy:

- Jane Jacobs, urban planner known for her groundbreaking study in 1961 titled *The Life and Death of Great American Cities,* recently wrote of a *Dark Age Ahead*. Jacobs identifies five central pillars crucial to our culture that are insidiously decaying: community and family, education, science and technology, government, and the professions.
- Taking a phrase from Tocqueville's book that described the mores of the American people—*Habits of the Heart*—Robert Bellah and a team of fellow sociologists, in a book by that title, analyze how our radical individualism threatens to undermine our capacity for commitment to one another in the public sphere.
- Robert Putnam, in *Bowling Alone,* documents how the voluntary associations that once held our nation together are disappearing, with Americans increasingly engaging in commerce, politics, entertainment, and religion on an individual basis.
- Kevin Phillips, in *Wealth and Democracy,* critiques the growing gap between rich and poor in America, and in the world at large, arguing that democracy cannot be sustained with such an economic imbalance.
- Cornel West, in *Democracy Matters,* identifies three modern dogmas that are putting democracy at risk in our country and the world: free-market fundamentalism, aggressive militarism, and escalating authoritarianism.
- Jane Mayer's carefully researched expose in *The Dark Side* tells of how, in response to the events of 9/11, we came precariously close to losing our democracy through a total concentration of unchecked power within the executive

branch.

3 Paul David Sholin (unpublished 2002).

4 Martin E. Marty with Jonathan Moore, *Politics, Religion, and the Common Good: Advancing a Distinctly American Conversation About Religion's Role in Our Shared Life* (San Francisco: Jossey-Bass Publishers, 2000), 37.

5 Andrew Delbanco, *The Real American Dream: A Meditation on Hope* (Cambridge, Massachusetts: Harvard University Press, 1999).

6 *Ibid*, 106.

7 Kevin Starr, "Scorning Public Life Is Shameful," *Los Angeles Times*, September 21, 2003, M2.

8 Alexis de Tocqueville, *Democracy in America,* trans. Arthur Goldhammer (New York: Library Classics, 2004), 509.

9 Matthew Spalding & Patrick J. Garrity, *A Sacred Union of Citizens: George Washington's Farewell Address and the American Character* (Lanham, MD: Rowman & Littlefield Publishers, 1996), 62 ff. The Farewell Address of September 19, 1796, is printed in its entirety as an Appendix; quotes are located on page 177-8.

Chapter 4: WHEN THE PEOPLE RULE: DEMOCRATIC VALUES

1 Thucydides, *The Peloponnesian War,* translated by Walter Blanco (New York: W.W. Norton & Co, 1998), 73.

2 *Ibid*, 227-31.

3 *Ibid*, 74.

4 Thomas Cahill, *Sailing the Wine-Dark Sea: Why the Greeks Matter* (New York: Nan A. Talese/Doubleday, 2003), 241. For yet a third translation of this sentence from "The Funeral Oration" see John Wallach below.

5 John R. Wallach, "Two Democracies and Virtue," ed. J. Peter Euben, John R. Wallach, and Josiah Ober, *Athenian Political*

Thought and the Reconstruction of American Democracy (Ithaca: Cornell University Press, 1994), 319.

6 *Ibid,* 330.

7 Glenn Tinder, *The Political Meaning of Christianity: An Interpretation* (Baton Rouge: Louisiana State University Press, 1989), 187.

8 Wallach, *op. cit.,* 332.

9 Robert B. Westbrook, *John Dewey and American Democracy* (Ithica: Cornell University Press, 1991), 79.

10 *Ibid,* 534.

11 Wallach, *op. cit.,* 333.

12 *Ibid,* 334.

13 While this popular saying attributed to the Christian apologist G. K. Chesterton is frequently used to make a point about the limitations of tolerance, it is questionable whether he said it. Chesterton himself was accepting of persons holding views contrary to his, but he had little patience with those who would not take a stand in the face of a moral challenge. As he actually said, "Impartiality is a pompous name for indifference, which is an elegant name for ignorance." ["Puritan and Anglican," *The Speaker,* December 15, 1900.]

Chapter 5: WHEN GOD IS SOVEREIGN: BIBLICAL VALUES

1 Howard Clark Kee, Franklin W. Young, and Karlfried Froehlich, *Understanding the New Testament* (Englewood Cliffs, New Jersey: Prentice Hall, 1965), 114.

2 Walter Brueggemann, *Theology of the Old Testament: Testimony, Dispute, Advocacy* (Minneapolis: Fortress Press, 1997), 736.

Chapter 6: PILGRIMS AND POLITICS

1 Alexis de Tocqueville, *Democracy in America,* trans. Arthur

Goldhammer (New York: Library Classics, 2004), 338.

2 Jon Butler, Grant Wacker & Randall Balmer, *Religion in American Life: A Short History* (New York: Oxford University Press, 2003), ix ff.

3 A cartoon I saw once while visiting the local Native American Center in San Bernardino leading up to a community-wide Thanksgiving service gives the alternative perspective of this American holiday. Picturing a small unsuspecting huddle dressed in black-garbed traditional outfits in the shadow of a huge boulder descending upon them from overhead, the caption reads: "When Plymouth Rock landed on the Pilgrims."

4 George Willison, *Saints and Strangers* (New York: Time-Life Books, 1945), 147.

5 *Ibid,* 152.

6 Williston Walker, *The Creeds and Platforms of Congregationalism* (Philadelphia: Pilgrim Press, 1960), 92.

7 Nathaniel Philbrick, *Mayflower* (New York: Viking Penguin, 2006), 352.

8 Sarah Vowell, *The Wordy Shipmates* (New York: Riverhead Books, 2008), 71-2.

9 Jon Butler, *Religion in Colonial America* (New York: Oxford University Press, 2000), 36.

10 Tocqueville, *op. cit.*, 39.

11 Butler, *op. cit.,* 54.

12 *Ibid,* 136.

13 A. James Reichley, *Faith in Politics* (Baltimore: Brookings Institution Press, 2002), 104.

14 This claim will be explored in more detail in Chapter 7.

15 Reichley, *op. cit.*, 54.

16 Conrad Cherry, ed., *God's New Israel: Religious Interpretations of American Destiny* (Englewood Cliffs, N.J.: Prentice Hall, 1971), 65.

17 H. Richard Niebuhr, *The Kingdom of God in America* (New

York: Harper & Row, 1937), 78 f.

Chapter 7: CALVIN AND THE CONSTITUTION

1 Isaac Kramnick and R. Laurence Moore, *The Godless Constitution: The Case Against Religious Correctness* (New York: W.W. Norton & Company, 1996), 27.

2 Alexis de Tocqueville, *Democracy in America,* trans. Arthur Goldhammer (New York: Library Classics, 2004), 39.

3 Ironically, the modern-day Tea Party Movement calling for a return to strict adherence to the U.S. Constitution actually stands in opposition to the spirit and substance of the Constitution itself. The TPM is more libertarian than republican.

4 John Calvin, *Institutes of the Christian Religion,* trans. Henry Beveridge (Edinburgh: Calvin Translation Society, 1846), Chapter 20, "On Civil Government," par. 8 and 3.

5 Reinhold Niebuhr, *The Children of Light and the Children of Darkness* (New York: Charles Scribner's & Sons, 1944), 17.

6 James Madison, *Federalist,* No. 51 [emphasis added].

7 I call these "leaks" not only as a literary device, but because I have not succeeded in substantiating the original sources for these quotes. They were included in a packet of resources distributed in 1975 by my denomination in preparation for the celebration of the U.S. Bicentennial. And they appear today online in *Brainy Quotes* (a surely unimpeachable source!).

8 Richard Hofstadter, *The American Political Tradition: And the Men Who Made It* (New York: Alfred A. Knopf, 1948), 5.

9 H. Richard Niebuhr, *The Kingdom of God in America* (Chicago: Willet, Clark & Co., 1937), 80.

10 Glenn Tinder, *The Political Meaning of Christianity: An Interpretation* (Baton Rouge: Louisiana State University Press, 1989), 10 [emphasis added].

11 *Ibid,* 178.

12 Reinhold Niebuhr, *op. cit.*, 9-12.
13 *Ibid*, xiii.

Chapter 8: A QUESTION OF PATERNITY

1 Paul Rogat Loeb, *Soul of a Citizen: Living with Conviction in a Cynical Time* (New York: St. Martin's Press, 1999), 16.
2 Saul Alinsky, *Reveille for Radicals* (New York: Random House, 1946), 15. See also Alinsky's *Rules for Radicals: A Practical Primer for Realistic Radicals* (New York: Random House, 1971). Written a quarter century after his first book, Alinsky expands upon his original ideas with a detailed description of the organizing process.
3 Ella Baker will be introduced more thoroughly in Chapter 10.
4 Stephen Hart, *Cultural Dilemmas of Progressive Politics: Styles of Engagement Among Grassroots Activists* (Chicago: The University of Chicago Press, 2001), 56.
5 *Ibid*, 55.
6 Mark R. Warren, *Dry Bones Rattling: Community Building to Revitalize American Democracy* (Princeton, N.J.: Princeton University Press, 2001), 45. Source of this quote is an interview with Harry Boyte, author of *Commonwealth: A Return to Citizen Politics*.
7 Benjamin E. Mays, *A Gospel for the Social Awakening: Selections from the Writings of Walter Rauschenbusch* (New York: Association Press, 1950), 48.
8 H. Richard Niebuhr, *The Kingdom of God in America* (New York: Harper & Row, 1937), 162.
9 Mays, *op. cit.* 47.
10 *Ibid*, 80-5.
11 *Ibid*,105.
12 H. R. Niebuhr, *op. cit.*, 164.
13 John A. Coleman, S.J., "The Future of Catholic Social Thought," *Modern Catholic Social Teaching*, ed. Kenneth R. Himes et al. (Washington, D.C.: Georgetown University

Press, 2005), 522-3.

14 Charles E. Curran, *Catholic Social Teaching 1891-Present: A Historical, Theological, and Ethical Analysis* (Washington, D.C.: Georgetown University Press, 2002), 7.

15 Coleman, *op. cit.*, 527.

16 Curran, *op. cit., 12.*

17 *Ibid,* 152.

18 *Ibid,* 133-7.

19 *Sollicitudo rei socialis,* as quoted by Curran, 134.

20 Coleman, *op. cit.*, 528.

Chapter 9: MORE BRANCHES ON THE FAMILY TREE

1 Jonah Pesner, "Will Synagogues Organize for Justice?" (*Sh'ma:* A publication of Jewish Family & Life, January 2007/Shevat 5767), 1.

2 Jonathan Sacks, *The Dignity of Difference: How to Avoid the Clash of Civilizations* (London/New York: Continuum, 2002), 201.

3 Michael Walzer, *Exodus and Revolution* (New York: Basic Books, 1985), 149.

4 Jonathan Sacks, *To Heal a Fractured World: The Ethics of Responsibility* (New York: Schocken Books, 2005), 75-6.

5 *Ibid*, 77.

6 *Ibid*, 82-3.

7 James H. Cone, *Black Theology and Black Power* (New York: The Seabury Press, 1969), 9.

8 James H. Cone, *Risks of Faith: The Emergence of a Black Theology of Liberation, 1968-1998* (Boston: Beacon Press, 1999), 43.

9 Cone, *Black Theology and Black Power*, 38.

10 Stokely Carmichael (Kwame Ture) with Ekwueme Michael Thelwell, *Ready for Revolution* (New York: Scribner, 2003), 513-4.

11 *Ibid*, 29.

12 Charles M. Payne, *I've Got the Light of Freedom: The Organizing Tradition and the Mississippi Freedom Struggle* (Berkeley: University of California Press, 1995), 364.
13 *Ibid,* 332.
14 Barbara Ramsby, *Ella Baker and the Black Freedom Movement: A Radical Democratic Vision* (Chapel Hill, NC: The University of North Carolina Press, 2003), 194.
15 *Ibid,* 417-8.
16 *Ibid,* 364.
17 "THE POWER OF NEW VOICES" (2003), a video produced by the PICO National Network.
18 Cornel West, *Race Matters* (New York: Vintage Books, 1994), 156.

Chapter 10: SELF-INTEREST 'PROPERLY UNDERSTOOD'

1 Reinhold Niebuhr, *The Children of Light and the Children of Darkness* (New York: Charles Scribner's Sons, 1944), 9.
2 Douglas Hofstadter, *I Am a Strange Loop* (New York: Basic Books, 2007)—as quoted by David Brooks, "A Partnership of Minds," *New York Times,* 7/20/07.

Chapter 11: POWERLESSNESS CORRUPTS

1 The meditation called "Power and Love" was in a packet of modern resources based on the *Spiritual Exercises* by Ignatius of Loyola used by a small group of men that met weekly for scripture and prayer.
2 Paul Tillich, *Love, Power, and Justice* (New York: Oxford University Press, 1960), 53.
3 Glenn Tinder, *The Political Meaning of Christianity: An Interpretation* (Baton Rouge: Louisiana State University Press, 1989), 240.
4 Walter Wink, *Engaging the Powers: Discernment and Resistance in a World of Domination* (Minneapolis: Fortress Press, 1992), 3-10.

5 Paulo Freire, *Pedagogy of the Oppressed,* trans. Myra Bergman Ramos (New York: Herder and Herder, 1971), 31-2.

6 *Ibid,* 34-5.

7 Tillich, *op. cit.,* 115.

8 Michael Lerner, *Surplus Powerlessness: The Psychodynamics of Everyday Life...and the Psychology of Individual and Social Transformation* (New Jersey: Humanities Press, 1991), 2. Chapter 1 of Lerner's book (pp. 2-19) is titled "Powerlessness Corrupts."

9 *Ibid.* Lerner makes a strong statement in defense of religion in chapter 19 (pp. *291-317).* He argues that "religious traditions ... can make an important contribution to a struggle against Surplus Powerlessness." In effect, he is saying that the experience of surplus powerlessness by congregations and clergy is an expression of a loss of faith. Feeling and acting more powerless than the actual power situation requires is the consequence of a failed relationship with the powerful sacred symbols that lie at the center of each faith tradition.

Chapter 12: RELATIONSHIPS THAT GO SOMEWHERE

1 Diarmuid O'Murchu, *Quantum Theology: Spiritual Implications of the New Physics* (New York: The Crossroad Publishing Company, 1997), 82.

2 Jacques Dupuis, *Toward a Christian Theology of Religious Pluralism* (Maryknoll, New York: Orbis Books, 1997), 385-90.

Chapter 13: VALUE-DRIVEN POLITICS

1 Jose′ Carrasco, for many years a part time consultant for PICO, more than anyone else has influenced my understanding of community organizing as being driven by values. I first encountered him in the early 1990s when he came to San Bernardino to do an exploratory training event with several congregations in the earliest stage of beginning

to consider community organizing. Professor Carrasco was one who taught primarily by the oral tradition rather than by publishing. His invaluable insights as an intellectual strategist and visionary into the organizing process, therefore, are what can be recalled by those of us fortunate to have been in his presence over the years. In the 1970s he worked with COPS, an IAF federation in San Antonio and helped to shape a new paradigm of congregation-based organizing. Subsequently he became PICO's teaching consultant. He was one of the primary persons in PICO to bring attention to the need for clergy support and development in their key role as leaders in faith-based community organizing. Jose′ Carrasco is now retired as professor of Chicano Studies at California State University, San Jose.

2 Richard L. Wood, *Faith in Action: Religion, Race, and Democratic Organizing in America* (Chicago: The University of Chicago Press, 2002), 164.

3 I am indebted to Jim Keddy, community organizer and longtime director of the statewide PICO California Project, for his excellent reflection on political ideology circulated in the network in December of 1998.

4 Some of Jose′ Carrasco's thinking is found in interviews conducted by Stephen Hart. See *Cultural Dilemmas of Progressive Politics,* pages 75-81, for an excellent summary of the discussion of values in organizing. This paragraph borrows substantially from Hart's reporting of his interviews with Carrasco.

5 Jim Ferrell, a professor of history and Director of American Studies at St. Olaf College, points out how "MasterCard takes the radical idea that we can have priceless moments without buying anything, and turns it into an occasion for spending. The company capitalizes on our idealism to sell us more materialism." [online reference]

6 Walter Brueggemann, *Theology of the Old Testament:*

Testimony, Dispute, Advocacy (Minneapolis: Fortress Press, 1997), 718-20.

Chapter 14: JESUS' ORGANIZING STRATEGY

1 The first sighting of this saying appears to be on Jonathan Martin's blog, 9/4/08 at 11:04 a.m. The evening prior, during the Republican Convention, both New York Mayor Rudolph Giuliani and Alaska Governor Sarah Palin made disparaging remarks about Senator Barack Obama's experience as a community organizer. Martin commented in response: "Mrs. Palin needs to be reminded that Jesus Christ was a community organizer and Pontius Pilate was a governor."

2 Mary Matalin & James Carville, *All's Fair: Love, War, and Running for President* (New York: Random House, 1994).

3 Barack Obama, *Dreams from My Father: A Story of Race and Inheritance* (New York: Crown Publishers, 1995), 272-295.

4 Richard A. Horsley and Neil Asher Silberman, *The Message and the Kingdom: How Jesus and Paul Ignited a Revolution and Transformed the Ancient World* (Minneapolis: Fortress Press, 1997), 51.

5 Excerpted from a reflection presented by the author at the PICO National Clergy Caucus held at Los Altos, California, October 26-29, 1998. Title: *Putting Faith into Action: Jesus' Strategic Plan for Mission.*

6 Robert W. Funk, Roy Hoover and the Jesus Seminar, *The Five Gospels: The Search for the Authentic Words of Jesus* (New York: Macmillan, 1993).

7 John Dominic Crossan, *The Historical Jesus: The Life of a Mediterranean Jewish Peasant* (New York: HarperCollins Publishers, 1991), 349.

Chapter 15: TELLING OUR STORY IN A NEW WAY: The Organizing Pastor

1 Heidi Neumark (referenced in chapter 2) is a master story-

teller. She demonstrates as well as anyone I know the concept developed here of the pastor as steward of the stories of the congregation and community.

2 Kevin M. Bradt, S.J., *Story as a Way of Knowing* (Kansas City: Sheed and Ward, 1997), x.

3 Richard L. Wood, *Faith in Action: Religion, Race, and Democratic Organizing in America* (Chicago: The University of Chicago Press, 2002), 78.

4 Martin Luther King, Jr., *Strength to Love* (New York: Harper and Row, 1963), 46.

5 *Ibid,* 64.

GENERAL INDEX

INDEX OF BIBLICAL CITATIONS

INDEX OF COMMUNITY ORGANIZING PRINCIPLES/APHORISMS

In the PICO National Network a number of "principles" have been generated spontaneously to articulate in simple terms basic elements of the organizing process. Several of these appear in this book as cited below. They are also referred to here as "aphorisms," a term used in biblical scholarship to refer to short sayings in the gospels. An aphorism is a pithy observation that contains a general truth. Hence...

The keystone of this book is the aphorism:

Additional principles/aphorisms: